LIVING WITCHERY
Divination

Living Witchery Divination

Edited by
Alexandra Tanet,
Kim Fairminer &
Sandra Greenhalgh

© copyright Byrning Tyger 2023
Each author is copyright owner of their own contributed materials.

The moral rights of the authors have been asserted.

All rights reserved. Except as permitted under the Australian Copyright Act 1968 (for example, a fair dealing for the purposes of study, research, criticism or review), no part of this book may be reproduced, stored in a retrieval system, communicated or transmitted in any form or by any means without prior written permission.

All inquiries should be made to the Publisher.

Printed in Australia.
Cover design by Kylie Sek.

Disclaimer

Views or opinions represented in this publication are personal and belong solely to the individual author. Although the editors and publisher have made every effort to ensure that the information in this book was correct at press time, the editor and publisher do not assume and hereby disclaim any liability to any party for any loss, damage, or disruption caused by errors or omissions, whether such errors or omissions result from negligence, accident, or any other cause.

Some names and identifying details have been changed to protect the privacy of individuals.

ISBN   978-0-6482701-6-4

www.byrningtyger.com

In the spirit of reconciliation, we acknowledge the Traditional Custodians of Country throughout Australia and their connections to land, sea, sky and community. We pay our respects to Elders past and present and future.

Table of Contents

Foreword 1
FORMING: Getting Started 3
   Divination: An Overview 5
      By Alexandra Tanet

   Developing Your Psychic Skills 11
      By Alexandra Tanet

   The Mystique of the Fortune Teller 19
      By Kim Fairminer

FUNDAMENTALS: Natural World 23
   Divination With Herbs 25
      By Ki-ian

   Ogham - Divinatory Language of Plants 39
      By Sandra Greenhalgh

FOUNDATIONS: Traditional Forms 49
   Divining With Horary Astrology 51
      By Kim Fairminer

   Scrying and Black Mirrors 62
      By Lisa-jane Mason

   Runes – Divination with Long Branches of the Younger Futhark 70
      By Miranda Kopittke

FACETS: Common or Folk 87
   Tassology – Tea Leaf Reading 89
      By Jacq Hackett

   It's All in Your Hands 96
      By Scarlet Paige

   Divinatory Dreaming 112
      By Kim Fairminer

   Folk Magic and the Art of Divination in Everyday Life 120
      By Scarlet Paige

FOCUS: Cards **129**
    Cartomancy 131
        By Sandra Lee

    Tarot and Divination 143
        By Linda Marson

    Oracle Cards 158
        By Sandra Greenhalgh

FLOURISH: Next Steps **165**
    Reading For Other People 167
    Professional Practicalities 173
    Being the Querent 181
References and Bibliography **185**
Acknowledgements and Credits **187**

Foreword

Welcome to *Living Witchery Divination*! Here you will learn about popular divination methods of Tarot cards, palmistry, tea leaf reading, astrology, and runes, as well as some lesser-known divination techniques. Have you tried making a black mirror and scrying with it? Or connected with plants to receive psychic insights? Learn about these methods and more.

We've also included suggestions about how to improve your psychic skills and become a professional reader, along with a wide range of other fascinating divination topics.

All authors are Australian with years of practical divination experience. As much as possible, we have anchored the content to this ancient and magnificent country, while understanding many aspects of divination are universal.

You may recognise some contributors from *Living Witchery Beginner Witch Guide*, and we are delighted to include chapters from some other knowledgeable friends of ours. It's difficult to be an expert in everything, which is why we enjoy being able to bring all this wisdom into one space.

Are you now wondering what intriguing topic to read first? We suggest that you be guided by your intuition and read chapters in whatever order you wish.

Bright blessings,
Alexandra, Kim, and Sandra

FORMING: Getting Started

Divination involves using our psychic skills or, put simply, being able to 'vibe stuff'. It is the practice of using intuition to glean hidden information and predict future events. Let's start by exploring some key themes around divination, including ethics, what it means to be psychic, and how to improve your intuition.

Divination: An Overview

By Alexandra Tanet

Every person has some form of psychic ability or intuition. You may have experienced eerily accurate 'gut feelings' or dreams that turn out to be true. Or perhaps you've received uncanny insights or have a deep fascination for divination tools such as Tarot. Maybe you are reading this book to improve your skills? Exploring divination is a worthwhile journey to undertake for many reasons.

Fortunately, there is no one way to practice divination or to 'be psychic'. The sky (and beyond!) is your limit and there is no rule book. Having said that, of course having some sound guidance – such as the information in this book – is helpful to provide some pointers along the way.

Psychic skills aren't heavily reliant on careful thinking or methodical analysis. Notice that 'divination' and 'divine' share the same Latin root word, *divinare,* which means to be inspired by a god. The art of divination involves connecting with the 'otherworlds', rather than using the physical senses of sight, smell, touch, hearing, and taste.

While tapping into our intuition, we use extrasensory perceptions of clairvoyance (seeing items or events which are distant in time and/or place), claircognisance (an innate knowing), clairaudience (hearing things which are inaudible), or clairsentience (experiencing feelings or perceptions). Less well known but also useful are clairolfaction (psychic smelling, sometimes called clairalience) and clairgustance (psychic tasting). Our psychic skills may rely on one or a combination of these senses.

Where do intuitive messages come from? Some people believe they are engaging with beings of greater intelligence or wisdom, while others think they are receiving guidance from their own higher self, or guides, angels, or ancestors. Maybe you prefer to seek guidance from a sparkly unicorn guide or a magical crystal. All these different options are valid, because as mentioned earlier, there is no rule book.

The benefits of divination

Divination is a core skill and everyday part of magical practice for many people in modern cultures, including those of us who are witches. Honing your psychic skills and divination ability will assist you to:

- ✦ Explore potential future opportunities and outcomes
- ✦ Integrate past experiences and circumstances
- ✦ Make decisions, and consider alternative choices
- ✦ Strengthen connections with otherworldly beings and realms
- ✦ Facilitate a sense of self-empowerment
- ✦ Help create a meaningful life and healthy relationships.

Divination offers a more holistic, non-logical approach to decision-making and problem-solving and is particularly beneficial within Westernised cultures, which tends to consistently prioritise intellect and logic as superior.

What's in a name?

There are many ways to divine. In this book, we use the word divination as an umbrella term for a range of practices, recognising there are differences and commonalities between modalities. While the word divination was historically linked with rituals involving deities or spirits, this definition has changed over time to be more encompassing.

Being psychic or intuitive seems to be pretty much the same thing, which is why we've used the words interchangeably. If you are practicing any form of divination, you are drawing upon your psychic/intuitive abilities.

There are a couple of common terms – medium and channeller – which seem mean the same thing, though there are subtle nuances. Mediumship involves being the intermediary for communications from people who have died or supernatural entities/spirits. Channelling also means being a link or conduit to a spiritual entity or otherworldly realms.

However, a key difference is that a channeller may go into a trance state, allowing a spirit entity to speak or act through them. It can become confusing trying to discern the difference between a 'psychic medium' and an 'intuitive channeller', if indeed there is one.

Diviners often use their tool or modality to describe their occupation or service, e.g. astrologer, Tarot card reader, scryer.

Tools

Many people immediately think of Tarot or tea leaves when it comes to divination, but that's just the beginning! Using a physical implement – which we refer to as a 'tool' in this book – can boost your divination abilities. Divination tools help to focus the reader, provide an energetic container, and enhance your readings with imagery and symbolism. I personally like using tools during a planned divination session. The process of working with the physical item helps me 'get in the zone' for the reading (i.e., change my consciousness). When I've packed away my tools, it's a clear sign that the session is closed.

Your divination tool need not be expensive. It just needs to work for you. You certainly aren't limited to one form of divination, although chances are you will settle on a favourite method. This book explores many useful options, some you may be familiar with, and others less commonly used, including runes, mirrors, plants, and everyday items.

> You do not have to be gifted your first set of Tarot cards.
> It's perfectly fine to use second-hand cards, and to sell or swap decks.

The challenges of divination

Before we get much further into our journey of discovery, let's consider the downsides of divination. Sadly, these exist. Due to the non-scientific nature of divination, it has a poor reputation in modern Westernised cultures. Divination is denigrated because it's not a consistently replicable process with 100% accurate outcomes. People who claim psychic abilities are often mocked by the media, in the workplace, and in social settings. Divination is gently ridiculed as being a bit 'woo woo' or condemned as being fake or a silly superstition. Currently, there are problems with Internet scammers claiming to be psychics, though all they want is your online identity and preferably your bank account details with it. It's almost enough to make you want to pack away your Tarot cards!

There's also the challenging concept of free will versus predestination (or fate) underlying the foundation of divination. Are we truly the independent champions of our own destiny? Or is everything that happens part of a grand plan, and we are merely pawns on a cosmic chessboard?

It's most likely that humans function with an uneven mix of both free will (i.e. future is completely changeable) and predestination (i.e. future is set and non-negotiable). It's also likely that we can change some things in our future if we know potential events in advance. Having foreknowledge gives us the option to adjust our actions to either embrace or avoid that potential future event. On the other hand, some things seem almost inevitable, as if nothing we do or say will make a difference. Divination is important because it assists people to become conscious of choices they make, and potentially change how they think or approach the world through everyday decisions.

To add another layer of complexity, some may have the perception that divination should only be used for deep personal reflection or self-awareness, rather than for mundane fortune telling. Even the word 'fortune teller' seems to be a slur, rather than a neutral description of someone engaged in a legitimate activity to ascertain the future, or to understand situations or relationships. I see no problem in using divination for the telling of 'fortunes' as well as for spiritual insights.

Ethics when reading for others

Practicing your divination skills can raise a host of ethical questions and sooner or later as a diviner reading for others, you are going to face some ethical dilemmas. Be prepared for situations that may make you feel a little uncomfortable. Imagining tricky scenarios in your head before they arise helps you work out your own feelings and develop ways of navigating the issue.

There are no absolute answers, as opinions vary widely. Everyone's spiritual, philosophical, moral, cultural, socio-economic background and experiences are unique, so it is impossible to give you a list of commandments that are never to be broken. In fact, if anyone is promoting rigid answers to ethical dilemmas, I'd suggest you ignore that advice as it is probably uninformed by the nuances of real-life experiences.

> Whatever you say in a reading bears more weight than an 'ordinary person' because you are likely to be perceived by your client as being 'gifted' with otherworldly talents, regardless of the truth of what it is to be psychic.

Accepting money for readings

One of the common ethical concerns is whether you should you charge money for readings. The bottom line is this is your decision. However, I would suggest not charging high rates while you are a beginner. In principle, the price of a divination reading should be indexed to experience and perceived accuracy as well as market price.

The first time you accept money for a reading will probably feel a little strange but that doesn't make it morally wrong. You've invested time, energy, and your own money to purchase your tools and learn your craft. In material terms, you are offering a service to another and deserve to be compensated for your efforts. There is also an argument to be made for keeping the Universe in balance by allowing money to flow as a form of energy exchange.

Reading about others without permission
Then there's the thorny question of whether you should read about others without explicit permission. I don't have an issue with doing this, as it's difficult to disentangle relationships or the impacts other people have on us. We are all social beings, with multiple connections between us.

However, the line between an admirer and a stalker isn't always clear, and it's a lot tidier to focus on the person sitting in front of you during a reading. To avoid inadvertently encouraging your client to interfere in the life of someone else, you may decide to ask the querent to rephrase their question or adapt the focus of your reading.

Death predictions
Should you tell someone if you believe they (or a loved one) is going to die soon? Generally speaking, no. Exceptions may be if you trust your skills to an extreme degree and think it might be helpful rather than harmful to share your feedback with the querent. Do you have the communication skills, compassion, and time to talk with the querent about a death forecast? Unless you do, perhaps exercise extreme caution before delivering a definitive forecast of someone's death.

Reading for children and young adults
Doing readings for or about a child or young person may bring up ethical concerns. Telling a parent that their child will be an international celebrity – or end up in jail – can create unintended consequences. How old is the child? Who is paying for the reading? If the child is present during the reading, you will need to adapt what you share to their developmental level. Whether the young person is present or not, leaving extra room for their free will and possibilities (rather than rigid predictions) is a sound ethical principle.

Refusing a question
Can you refuse to answer a querent's questions? Or refuse to do a reading for someone? Yes, you certainly can. However, if you are professionally reading on behalf of someone's business, an outright refusal can get tricky. It's useful to have strategies in place to help you handle the situation when (or if) it arises.

What if the querent is under the influence of mind-altering substances or seems highly disturbed when they arrive for their session? Or you get a strong psychic message to avoid the encounter? What will you say to this client who you don't want to read for? Have they paid for the reading in advance, and do you have the option to process an immediate refund? Having a short, pre-rehearsed response will help you handle the situation with confidence.

About Alexandra Tanet

Alexandra Tanet is the nom de plume for a Brisbane witch who prefers to keep a low profile on electronic and social media. She cast her first spell as a teenager and has been involved in facilitating Southeast Queensland covens for over 25 years. Alexandra is co-founder and co-High Priestess of The Circle Coven, Brisbane's largest, longest-running witch coven.

Alexandra is the author of Living Witchery: Coven, *the first book in the Living Witchery series. She is author and co-editor of* Living Witchery: Beginner Witch Guide *(published in 2021).*

Developing Your Psychic Skills

By Alexandra Tanet

Enhancing your psychic skills and intuition will help improve your divination readings. Some people are lucky to have strong psychic abilities which emerge naturally in childhood and continue to develop into adulthood. However, most of us have suppressed our innate abilities, often due to feedback from other people (usually parents and caregivers) or unpleasant experiences. The good news is we can improve our skills and abilities through focus and practice.

Try different activities to see what works best for you, and don't be afraid to experiment. Not everything is going to be a resounding success at first and that is OK. As with all things in life, you will periodically hit obstacles and experience frustrations. When this happens, return to a place of receptivity and ease. Roll with it. Trust. This is an exciting process of exploration and all part of the magic that is unfolding.

Start from where you are

Chances are you already have one psychic talent that is naturally more developed than others. Perhaps you have a knack for finding lost items? Maybe you can sense whenever someone is putting on a brave face? Maybe you recognise omens in the natural world? Or have regular moments of 'just knowing'?

Use this natural talent as an entry point. Draw upon your strengths and consider ways you can experiment, extend, or apply it in a different context. For example, if you identify as an empath and have a natural ability to share the emotional experience of loved ones, try connecting with animals such as birds, lizards, or a cat. What is that like? How is it similar? How is it different? If you enjoy scrying with a flame, try a different tool, like the black mirrors explored in the Foundations section. Or if you receive clear psychic visions, why not sketch them on paper or create digital art?

Follow your intuition

When you're listening to the unseen worlds, 'go live' with the information you receive. For example, the next time you get the urge to take a particular street or call a certain person, follow through on the feeling. At first you will probably feel a bit silly doing things that don't make rational sense. Soon though you will begin to experience more strange and wonderful coincidences which would never have happened if you didn't act on the intuitive information you received.

You may feel drawn to a particular tool or method which you know nothing about. Why not give it a try? As you are exploring new psychic abilities, don't be afraid to move out of your comfort zone and try something new.

Bond with your tools

First and foremost, spend time with your chosen divination tool (if you use one). Form a relationship with your tool. Pop it near your bed and carry it in your pocket or bag (if practical). Whatever tool you choose to use, learn it thoroughly. Do your research until you feel you are about to burst with knowledge. Then it's time to ignore the texts and focus on the inner-spirit connection you need for a good divinatory reading. At times, clear intuitive messages will override the 'face reading' of any tool you use.

Look after your tools. Treat them well as they are a vessel of divine intelligence. For example, I often ask people to wash their hands before touching my well-loved deck of Tarot cards to keep them clean. Before you pack your tool away, perform a simple visualisation to psychically cleanse it. My favourite technique for doing this with Tarot or oracle cards is to flick across the ends of the cards while imaging any stray energies flying off into the ether.

Create calm

Create a learning environment which is peaceful, calm, and private. With more experience, you can perform a reading in any setting, but it's easier to get started in a familiar and safe environment conducive to divination.

In a serene environment, it's easier to listen for the 'still, quiet voice' of genuine intuitive messages. This 'voice' is frequently muffled, or hollered over by the clamour of everyday thoughts and feelings. Being overstimulated also closes you off from these clear, quiet messages. Feeling relaxed and calm – and/or being in a place to inspire those feelings – can help.

Timing and seasonal influences

Learn about the times of day – or lunar or seasonal cycles – when your psychic senses seem to flow more easily. For some people this is late at night when others are sleeping. Samhain (late April to early May in Australia) is often a magical time for divination. Performing divination on the cusp between the old and new calendar year is another liminal opportunity. Some people find the new moon and/or full moon also sparks their intuitive senses. Keeping a diary can help you track when your psychic receptivity is high.

Meditate and visualise

Meditate. *Living Witchery: Beginner Witch Guide* includes useful information about meditation, changes of consciousness, as well as shielding and grounding. It's good magical hygiene to protect and shield yourself and the area before a reading, and then ground yourself afterwards. As we say in the coven (and in the country) if you open a closed gate, make sure you close it again.

The process may include visualising yourself 'unlinking' from your querent when the reading has finished, though this needn't be an elaborate or time-consuming process.

Try practicing energy centre (chakra) activities. Visualise your psychic abilities as being like water flowing through the energy centre at the centre of your brow (your 'third-eye chakra'). Maintain the flow as a gentle trickle. Then fully open the aperture and let the energy gush like water being released from a brimming dam. To finish, visualise the flood gates (third eye chakra) closing to minimise the flow. The more you practice opening and closing your psychic senses through these simple magical techniques, the more efficient and proficient you become.

Practice predictions purposefully

Practice makes almost perfect. Practice your readings with your friends, family, workmates, and spontaneous volunteers. Good, bad, and mediocre readings all help you become a better reader.

As you go about your day, try to predict seemingly random incidental events such as:

- which lift (elevator) will arrive first
- what colour car you will see at the next crossing
- what clothing a friend, family member, or workmate will wear

- the shape of the next cloud you see in the sky
- what card comes next after shuffling a deck of playing cards
- the location of an empty parking space.

Before visiting a new place (such as a friend's house, a restaurant, or park) try to visualise it. Imagine the colours, layout, and design, and write down these details so you can compare when you arrive at the venue.

Try to predict some significant or longer-term events such as political themes, births, deaths, marriages, or relationship breakups. Use a diary to record these, so you can look back later for accuracy and timing. You may realise that it's quite difficult to set accurate timeframe, unless perhaps you are an astrologer. I've received multiple readings where I was given quite specific timelines, with the predicated events occurring five to ten years later. Oops.

Look for signs and synchronicities

Often, there are hidden meanings associated with seemingly chance occurrences which only later reveal their significance. Sometimes, the messages from the otherworlds are obvious and not easily ignored. At other times, what may seem of vital importance turns out to be a random event with minimal meaning. The challenge is to work out which is which, and this may not be apparent until hours or days after seeing the sign or synchronicity. Try keeping an open mind but err on the side of caution. Not everything means something.

Tune into your body

Learn how it feels when your readings or predictions are accurate. Is there a buzz? Do you just *know* that the messages you are receiving are spot-on? Is the quiet intuitive voice speaking clearly to you? I generally get the tingles when there's something particularly magical occurring during a reading. I suddenly develop goose bumps up and down my body, and sometimes the querent also experiences this at the same time.

Tune into your bodily sensations or 'gut instincts.' How does it feel when you are about to text a friend, and they text you first? How does it feel when you randomly receive predictions which turn out to be true? Are you experiencing tension in any part of your body? Or do you have a sense of lightness, rightness, or relaxation? Dig a bit deeper and reflect on possible meanings for this. What is your body trying to tell you?

You may like to try adopting a vegan or vegetarian diet, or gently fast to enhance your psychic abilities. This can free energy expended on digestion and aids their divination skills. Other people find a hefty boost of caffeine helps, so this is very much down to individual preferences.

Slip into the zone
Repetitive movements or semi-hypnotic activities such as walking, stretching, craft work, jigsaw puzzles, or mopping the floor may entertain your consciousness and help release your psychic flow. I have 'car park moments', when I've received extremely useful messages while laboriously driving up the multiple levels of my familiar workplace car park. Slowly driving the routine route seems to put me into a mild state of relaxation where problems are (seemingly) miraculously solved. What are your own 'car park moments?'

Try to learn about your personal times of liminality when your everyday mind switches off. Perhaps it could be linked to the elemental energies of Water, when you shower, or cross a bridge, or are up to your elbows in sudsy dishwater? Perhaps it occurs when you are gazing into a flame (Fire), kneading bread, or holding a special rock or crystal (Earth), or burning a particular incense (Air)?

Find a teacher
Eventually you may decide to look for a teacher or take formal lessons. This can be a useful way to disrupt individual habits, as a skilled teacher will be experienced with the learning trajectory. Having developed their own psychic skills over many years, a good teacher has personal experience of the bumps along the way. They will also be attuned to your needs and the needs of the class as a whole and adapt their teaching accordingly.

Who can help you along this journey of discovery? If you live in or near a town or city, sometimes there are in-person courses available. These may be advertised via esoteric or new age bookstores, or in alternative lifestyle magazines. Online social networks (such as Facebook or Meetup) can help you find local events or groups as well as experienced practitioners who provide lessons and mentoring. Another option is to attend a meeting at your local Spiritualist church, as these usually include a mediumship demonstration.

While lessons are a fun way to meet like-minded people, learn new techniques, and accelerate your skills, you will also need to practice regularly on your own – preferably every day.

> Don't pay extraordinarily large sums of money to receive teachings which claim to improve your intuition.
> High price doesn't necessarily mean best value.

Formalise your feedback

Although we know divination is not 100% accurate, it's useful to factor in some form of evaluation and reflection process, so you can continue to improve. Ways to do this include:

- ✦ Ask for feedback from your querents at the end of the divination session.
- ✦ Aim to validate the messages or insights you receive. Did the predicted event happen? Keep records and check your diary.
- ✦ Be aware of reader bias. Sometimes you will believe that the reading meant something, and on later reflection find that there is a completely different slant to the message. For example, consider the phrase, 'successful legal outcome.' Who is deemed to be successful, the plaintiff or defendant?

Self-care

When learning or enhancing any magical skill, maintaining healthy boundaries is vital for your mental and emotional wellbeing. It's easy to become addicted to parting the veil to the otherworlds at the expense of your physical and psychological wellbeing. Frequent or intensive divination practice can sometimes make it difficult to determine what is what is real and what is not. There's also an indistinct line between uncontrollably receiving intuitive messages and deteriorating with an undiagnosed or poorly managed mental health condition.

An unhealthy level of engagement with the liminal spaces of divination is often associated with a decline in your ability to function in the mundane world. Are you still paying the bills? Are you taking care of your body? Are you getting enough quality sleep? Are you maintaining social connections at work, or with family or friends? Are you able to safely disconnect from extra sensory messages, images, sounds or feelings? Are you feeling OK?

If you answered 'no' to any of the above questions and are worried about your wellbeing – or your loved ones are worried about you – take a break. Talk about the situation to someone you know and trust. For additional support, speak to a healthcare professional.

If you identify as an empath, make a conscious effort to protect and control your energetic integrity. Learn how *not* to take in or experience the feelings and emotions of other people. Whether you're an empath or not, learn to say 'no'. There is no rule that says you are obliged to receive random psychic messages 24/7.

And don't forget to drink lots of water. It helps to minimise the risk of a third-eye headache.

Relax
The final bit of advice is to relax! Sometimes it's just better to go with the flow, have a laugh, and follow your instincts. Don't be too serious or become fixated, as you may then experience psychic blocks instead of alignments. If you feel that a particular exercise is unduly onerous, it likely won't help you. Feel free to experiment, be creative, and have fun while you enhance your psychic skills in your own way.

Psychic senses power-up spell
The night before full moon, leave a glass of water in the moonlight. This can be inside on the windowsill or outside. The next morning, cover and remove the glass of moon-charged water before the sun reaches full power.

The following night (when it's full moon), take the glass of moon water, a candle and a lighter to a private space where you won't be disturbed. Light the candle and place the glass of moon water in front of it.

Enter a calm and reflective meditative state. Image you can see all, know all, and understand all.

Dip the little finger of your non-dominant hand into the moon water and draw a spiral on your forehead.

Say aloud some words that articulate your desire to improve your psychic ability. Here are some examples:

Day by day,
night by night,
my psychic skills
become more bright.

With the blessings of the moon and water and the power of the sun and flame,
my intuition and psychic skills become greater and more accurate every day.
So mote it be!

I spy with my third eye
things not normally seen.
By moon, by sun, by water and flame,
I walk the ways between.

Blow out the candle. Ground yourself by eating and drinking.

You can repeat this spell daily for a full lunar cycle until the next full moon, then tip out the remainder of the moon water onto a cherished plant.

About Alexandra Tanet

Alexandra Tanet is the nom de plume for a Brisbane witch who prefers to keep a low profile on electronic and social media. She cast her first spell as a teenager and has been involved in facilitating Southeast Queensland covens for over 25 years. Alexandra is co-founder and co-High Priestess of The Circle Coven, Brisbane's largest, longest-running witch coven.

Alexandra is the author of Living Witchery: Coven, *the first book in the Living Witchery series. She is author and co-editor of* Living Witchery: Beginner Witch Guide *(published in 2021).*

The Mystique of the Fortune Teller

By Kim Fairminer

Chances are you already have a stock character pictured in your head when I write of a diviner, a fortune teller, a psychic. She is a woman. She's sitting at table covered with a cloth and in front of her are her tools of the trade – a crystal ball, a deck of cards, or a Ouija board. She's young, she's pretty, she's wearing clothing that hints at her bohemian lifestyle. She's a little bit saucy and sexy, wouldn't you say?

Victorian imagery of fortune tellers persists as the archetype in people's minds, often incorporating mysterious heritage, headscarves, and hoop earrings. Some diviners perpetuate this image as a marketing gimmick, often veering into racist stereotypes, cultural appropriation, and dubious ethical decisions. I suggest you steer clear of any diviner marketing themselves in this way.

None of the people who have contributed to this book look anything like this archetypal fortune teller. All are experienced in the divinatory arts and offer a breadth of knowledge, from across continents and cultures and time.

And yet, our idea of a diviner, a fortune teller, a psychic is trapped in a Victorian time warp. It was a fascinating period with the rise of spiritualism, seances, and controversial personalities such as Aleister Crowley and Helena Blavatsky, and continues to be influential in alternate spiritualities in the English-speaking world.

The archetype of the fortune teller is as risqué now as she was then. She still captures the imagination of the modern world, particularly among women and non-binary people who are seeking empowerment in a cultural paradigm that continues to deny them self-determination and authority. No wonder her occupation has been besmirched and ridiculed for centuries. She was independent and made her own money, probably chose not to marry, and ignored a host of other social expectations.

The commercial exchange, so intimately connected to our experience of divination, is an important clue. Divination operates at the intersection of the material and spiritual worlds. Science and capitalism rely upon the complete separation of these realms, if not the annihilation of the world of spirit entirely. And that's without even mentioning the commercial interests of the culturally dominant religion.

Modern diviners – and seekers of divine wisdom – walk a similar path parallel to mainstream knowledge and decision-making processes. Most of the population will either actively dismiss the intuitive insights, gloss over them, or simply pretend they don't exist. They'll seek guidance when they feel lost or confused or empty but will revert to their materialist philosophy when the uncomfortable symptoms of soul disturbance have abated. As a diviner, you may find yourself fetishized as 'special' for your 'gifts' and thus (partially) forgiven for any social deviance. Such is the path of the witch.

Even among metaphysical practitioners, there's contention around the ethics of fortune (future) telling. Though frequently inaccurate, weather forecasts and economic outlooks are widely followed, accepted, and relied upon to make decisions which have a tangible impact on one's health and security. Telling the future is risky. Even in modern times, it can be a matter of life and death. Making predictions about the future is dangerous. The present moment is 'safe' and we're told we are free to do with it what we will. Interestingly, delving into the past seems to be morally neutral.

Divination is about the future. Even if you prefer to skirt around it, the decisions you make today – even a renewed perspective on the past – will affect your tomorrow.

So, what about 'real life' diviners, my witchy friends, the wonderful authors who contributed to this book? While some of us are partial to a scarf and costume jewellery, you probably won't notice us as we queue behind you at the post office. Magical people are surprisingly ordinary. Psychic abilities are amazing and they're also incredibly normal. You're just as likely to have a vision while doing the dishes as you are when slinging cards.

As you'll read in the contributor chapters, some families, and traditions of witchcraft pass on their divinatory knowledge within those groups. But, excluding closed cultural practices, don't think for a second that you need certain ancestry, or to be a hereditary witch, or be initiated in a particular path, or have a certificate of attainment to engage with the unseen worlds through divination.

Let go of the stereotypes and be curious. It's easy to make divination part of your everyday life – by sharing dreams with your household at breakfast, by pulling a 'card of the day', by listening to the trees on your afternoon walk.

There are messages all around you, all the time – even in that tedious post office queue – but not every insect that infiltrates your house is a messenger of the gods.

Be open but sceptical when you seek divination services from another. It's easy to deify the words of the diviner and in doing so surrender your own agency. As the client, you always retain power over your life and your decisions. Don't let your agency waft away in a cloud of incense and some mystical marketing campaign. No matter how many generations back this reader goes, if the information they're offering doesn't empower you to make positive choices in your life, they're not helping.

Whether you are the client or the diviner, do not be seduced and hypnotised by the mystique of the fortune teller.

To divine is to be of service – to yourself, to your friends and family, to clients. By stepping into this world, you are charged with the sacred responsibility to be of service to your fellow humans, to help them navigate life's tough decisions, to ease the burdens of the past, to unveil new opportunities for growth and flourishing.

Yes, you walk the ageless path of seers. You will also be helping people make regular life decisions – about money, love, health, work. It's magical and it's wonderfully ordinary.

Embark upon your divinatory journey with wonder and humility.

About Kim Fairminer

Kim is an astrologer, writer, and witch with more than 20 years hands-on experience as a magical practitioner. She has been a member of The Circle Coven for over ten years, including six years in the role of High Priestess. Before her life-changing midlife transits, she was an editor for a multinational company. She is author and co-editor of Living Witchery: Beginner Witch Guide *(published in 2021), writes horoscopes and forecasts for a range of publications, and shares esoteric wisdom in her online community. Kim writes, stargazes, and circle-casts from her home in suburban Brisbane.*

You can learn more about her work at kimfairminer.com

FUNDAMENTALS: Natural World

Many ancient divination practices were associated with the natural world. The techniques in this chapter focus on plants and your local surroundings.

Divination With Herbs

By Ki-ian

As a young child I grew up in the emerging ecology of urban Sydney, the concrete jungle. Going bush was a regular thing we did. I remember excitedly helping pack the car. Tent, airbeds, one bag limit each, bedding, towels and loads of blankets. We always seemed to go south in the winter months. There was something about cold weather and campfires.

The long drive down the coast roads was accompanied by fights with my brothers in the car. It was usually August (Imbolc) and I marvelled at the smiling warmth that blossomed from the golden wattle flowers at the roadside. They were like a welcoming hug as we turned inland to our remote camp.

No running water. No fast food. Just an open fire, early bedtime and rising with the sun for three nights, with the promise of a soft drink and a Sunday pub lunch on our way home.

We'd land at our camp, and I'd observe Dad choosing the best place for the tent. On one of our first trips, I was busting to go to the loo and looked at him, looked around and asked where the toilets were. He gave me a sweet smile, a shovel, and some toilet paper: "Take this, walk for about 50 steps that way, go a little bit off the path and dig a hole. Don't sit on the prickly plants."

It was so hugely scary! Here I was, no more than 10 years old heading into the bushland on my own. I gingerly counted the steps and remember finding a log and choosing to sit there for a while. It was one of the first times I felt fear, awe, devotion, love, and reverence for nature. A small wren came and squawked at me, and I recall seeing a large ironbark and spotting sap oozing out of the tree at my eye level. I gingerly reached out and its sticky edge stuck to my fingers like glue. Under my feet was a mix of native grasses, rocks, and leaves. I could see the tiniest of ants busy on their way with a focus and intent. They worked as a team, moving food, seed, and materials from one place to another. I remember wondering why humans didn't support each other more.

So much could get done if we just all got in and did it together.

I must have spent a while there, sitting on my log and observing, as Dad came to look for me. He asked, "what are you doing?" and I felt a little cranky – as if my conversation with the tree, grass, sap, ants, and wren had been rudely interrupted. I was called to head back and support – just as those ants were – setting up camp and orienting ourselves to our place for the next three days. There were things to do, and I was a part of the wider ecology that would impact the site for this short while.

The aromas of the Australian bush still linger. I can close my eyes and connect to that experience at any time; the sensory moment was so strong. This is where I see now that my journey with plants and nature awakened into more than observation. It moved into relationship.

This was my first relationship, conversation if you will, with Country. I felt so very safe and held. It was the first of many to come.

You may be wondering, "This is a book on divination. Why am I reading about relationship?"

Divination and relationship are a partnership that go hand in hand. Divining in nature is the capacity to observe and interact with the space and interpret the signs, symbols, and findings. To sit in nature itself will lead you to a 'knowing'. You will find and hear warning signs, conversations, be told of an approaching predator or danger, discover a wonderous moment of connection through a precious mineral or rock. You may see a shape or sign in a rockface which speaks out to you or answers your question. By acknowledging and engaging in our relationship with the land and nature, we begin a journey to better understand ourselves.

This is divination. We divine ourselves. We find ourselves. When using herbs as a divinatory tool, we speak into the ethers of nature and sit. We sit in innocence like that little girl on a log in the bush and we wait for a sign. In reciprocity we exchange and grow, harvesting our findings, and opening to wisdom and guidance.

Experientially, this is my prayer.

This chapter's intention is to share how four commonly used herbs can support us to find these markers on the map, provide that point on the compass. Here I will be aligning four herbs with the earth and moon cycle. These herbs correspond with times of stillness, planting, growth, and harvest alongside new, half, full and waning moons. Each earth and moon cycle holds an intent and focus. This framework supports us to learn to use these herbs as divinatory tools.

To distil ourselves. To discover ourselves. This is Living Witchery.

Relationships with herbs

The herbs chosen for this chapter are just the beginning of a wonderous path. Every herb you can possibly think of has potential for divination. Every plant and herb has a voice, soul, and (potentially) a desire to communicate. Every herb can be used on a deeper level. The path begins with plant communication. It begins with meditation. It begins in stillness.

To have a conversation with a plant for the purpose of divination is where we begin. The conversation takes form in many ways. Though I use the words 'plant communication', I first began to *listen* for the plant's words. I was waiting for the plant to actually speak to me.

Nothing.

As I sat and quietened my mind more and more, I realised I was looking for an anatomical response from something that did not have the same anatomy as me. I read and learned that I needed to notice other forms of communication. I sat some more and realised the importance (and efficiency) of truly listening to the plant. This included sight, sound, taste, aroma and of course, energy.

In terms of divination, and getting to know my chosen plant entirely, I begin by looking at the anatomy and physiology of the herb I intend to use. Its root system, leaves, stem, and structure. I dive deep into its nuances. The rose's thorn, the scent of mugwort as I brush the leaves, the vibrancy of the Lion's Tail flower, or the complexity of the passionflower.

Each of these nuances is the beginning of the divination process. It is where I start to understand the herb and what wisdom it may offer. Shadow and light. Help and harm. The rose is a herb of the heart, yet the thorn can draw blood. The mugwort, as the crone herb, communicates clearly and strong in the form of a pungent aroma. The Lion's Tail flower dutifully shares its promise, inviting us to look directly into its complex petals where wisdom may be found. Maybe when we're seeing, we observe passionflower's tendrils reach out to seductively wind themselves around where they need to go, finding the path of least resistance. Relaxing us and guiding us to where we need to be.

Exercise

Choose a herb. If possible, sit alongside it. What do you see? What shape is the stem? The leaf? When you touch it, does it feel sticky or smooth? Is it sharp with thorns? Does it have an aroma? How does it make you feel? Draw the herb in your Book of Shadows. Write your findings around this drawing. Allow the aroma, feel, touch and (if safe) taste of the herb to guide your words.

Let it speak to you. This is the beginning of divining. The observation and listening at this point is the beginning of the plant communicating with you.

> *Salvia apiana* (white sage) in my herb garden has a huge boss vibe. It absolutely lets me know when to harvest, weed, whether to distil or dry, even how to sell it (e.g., as incense or loose leaf). I guarantee that just after I've followed this plant's instructions, the right buyer turns up and takes the lot. This is just one example of plant communication and listening to the wisdom of the 'green bloods'.

Divinatory herbs

As we mentioned earlier, all herbs have capacity to be used in divination practices. All herbs should be respected for the most impactful or subtle offerings. The humble rosemary supports remembrance and can clear the mind, easing anxiety and allowing clarity. The touch of a yarrow leaf will inspire comfort and yet its fibrous offering may speak to you of resilience and strength.

Don't forget the 'lesser' herbs (for the record, I don't like this phrase). Don't get caught up in the groove of the gloriously beautiful herbs, the bright and shining ones who are enjoying almost rock stardom and forget the knowing available in more humble herbs. Kitchen witchin' is a strong practice. Our ancestors utilised what they had around them, observed their surroundings and used nature to divine. The message that we gain from the humble rosemary can be just as profound as any other herb, and often is where we find the pearls of wisdom.

Having spoken about the light, ease, and subtlety of herbs, it would be irresponsible of me not to speak of the shadow side. Be cautious. Do you own research by comparing a range of reputable non-affiliated sources. Some of these herbs come with clear warnings and contraindications. Have agency in what you are trying out and when. Be mindful all the way from sourcing the herbs (particularly if you are wildcrafting) to harvesting, drying, processing, and using. Each of these steps are a part of our overall divination process, part of our magic, and a rushed moment not only can prove dangerous to you, but it will also be an opportunity missed. A communication or message gone.

The four herbs we are about to dive into can be found either by wildcrafting, purchased at your local herb nursery, or harvested from that wonderful garden you spotted on your daily walk (asking permission first of course!). I've chosen these herbs – or did I? I suspect they've chosen me! – as they're accessible, safe and support us to take the first step into divining with herbs.

There is a 'makings' section in each herb profile and it's here I've made some assumptions. I'm assuming you are grounded, have prepared for your ritual, and have your divining focus sorted and ready to go. Even better, that you've been sitting with your question for a while and are ready. As we get into making the different herbal goodness, this focus follows you. It's with you as you make your herbs, prepare your body oils, blends, teas, or smoke. It is with you as you bring your working through its full cycle.

Remember, we follow the cadence of nature and go slow. Ground. Focus. Centre. Clear your mind as I invite you to begin your plant divination journey.

Herb: Mugwort (*Artemesia vulgaris*)
Moon: Waning/dark moon
Earth: Mulch/compost
Essence: Surrender/stillness

We begin our divinatory plant journey in darkness. The time of stillness at the dark moon. The underworld and the point of deep surrender.

Mugwort supports us to walk between worlds. They offer us an opportunity to divine from a lucid state of neither here nor there. It is said that the goddess Artemis' divine presence is imbued throughout the plant. A keeper of wisdom and knowing, this herb is perfect for divining through our dreaming realms. Mugwort's magic and potency increases as it grows and flowers. A herb belonging to the moon goddess is the perfect place to begin our divinatory journey.

Monograph
Common names: Mugwort, common wormwood, sailor's tobacco
Latin name: *Artemisia vulgaris*
Plant family: Compositae
Parts used: Leaves (tips and tops)
Botany: A common perennial plant which grows up to two meters high, the dark green leaves have alternate pointed edges. Their underside is white/grey in colour and the flower and seed clusters present in the upper part
of the plant.
Harvesting: Harvest mugworts' tips and tops only, leaving the woody stems and lower leaves to the compost and garden offerings. Be selective. Be clear. Mindfully share the intent and purpose of your divination process. Be with the plant as you harvest. Let the plant know what you will be making (tea or smoke blend?) and the question for your divination.

Active constituents: The volatile oils of cineole and thujone pack a lot of punch in this herb.
Contraindications: Do not use if you are, or suspected to be, pregnant. Mugwort is an emmenagogue (brings on bleeding). Use with care.

Makings – tea and smoke
Harvest the young leaves and tie with a light cotton or hemp thread. Hang in an open area and allow to completely dry.

Once dried, reduce the herb by crushing in your hands (with your intent and divination question at the forefront of your mind) and place into a sealed container. Your end production is the size of tea leaves. Add one teaspoon per cup of hot water to your teapot or cup. This will do the trick to make the perfect dream tea. You can sweeten to taste with honey if you so desire. Strain and drink before bed.

Mugwort can also be added to sacred smoke mixes and blends well with other herbs. Another (more subtle) way to enjoy the herb is to place some of your dried mugwort into a dream pillow. Mugwort also makes an amazing smoke-cleanser. Opportunities for lucid dreaming and divining can be gained from all these ways of enjoying this herb.

Do not use with great frequency. I think of mugwort like a dear wise crone I am going to visit for a few days every now and then. This is the energy with which I use the herb. A short visit, we dive deep, and much wisdom is gained. Then it's time to leave and I put the herb away to wait for another day. Mugwort will lose its potency if used too often. Crone wisdom deserves respect and reverence. This is how I approach mugwort both in the garden and dreaming.

Herb: Lion's Tail
Moon: New moon
Earth: Prepare/feed
Essence: Vibration/begin

Out of the dark moon, we begin to prepare our ground and surrounds, feed our souls and selves bringing in the essence of vibration and beginnings of the new moon.

I first met this divine looking herb as I walked down the paddock and there it was, flowering in all its absolute glory, which to me describes the purpose and potential of this plant. It had been planted there by a dear witch friend and offered to the land. I am ever grateful for that offering and that witch (you know who you are).

Just as the new moon appears on the horizon, these flowers appear out of the green cocoon of their base, at first a suggestion of colour and then a bloom of striking beauty. A perfect herb to begin divination into the new moon period, to gain insight as we look towards new opportunities and growth. As we flow towards this part of the cycle, what a beautiful plant ally to have alongside us.

You can source the plant from your local nursery and/or the dried material from many online shops. I've provided my recommended retailers in Australia in the resources section of this book. We'd all love to grow as many herbs as we can, yet with this one, let's face it, not everyone has space for a two-metre bush in their front yard!

Either way, ensure you look for 'ethically wildharvested' or 'regeneratively grown' or 'organic' statements on the provider's website. Ask your seller where and how it was grown. As with anything we put on or in our body, or breathe in, it's important to know its origin.

This plant has mild psychoactive properties and, as with every other herb, should be used with reverence and care.

Monograph

Common Names: Wild dagga, hottentot tobacco, or lion's ear
Latin Name: *Leonotis leonorus*
Plant Family: Lamiaceae
Parts Used: Leaves and flowers
Botany: This large evergreen plant grows 1–2 metres tall and between 50 to 100 cm wide. The dark green leaves are held in opposite positions on its square stem. Lanceolate shaped, the leaves range from 2–10 cm long and can be quite thin, curve downward and may have spiky edges or toothed margins. The flowers are grouped in tiered whorls spiralling around the stem into attractive clusters. Native to South Africa, lion's tail has been naturalised in Australia.
Active constituents: Flavonoids, alkaloids, marrubiin (this is what makes it taste bitter)
Contraindications: Not to be used during pregnancy.

Makings - loose incense

For me, lion's tail is a subtle herb and the makings offered for this cycle are gentle yet transformative. Here we have a recipe for a loose incense blend to be used in our new moon rituals supporting divination and visioning. You can also use lion's tail flowers sprinkled through your smoke-cleansing wands. They are a glorious colour!

You'll need:
- ¼ part Lion's Tail flowers (dried)
- ¾ part Australian sandalwood
- A sprinkle of dried rose petals

Place your Australian sandalwood in your grinder and mill until it forms a fine powder. Think about the grounding of your new moon intention. Where is it anchored? Imagine the deep roots of the sandalwood tree holding your affirmation solidly in the earth's surface.

Gently open the lid and mindfully add the lion's tail flowers. You are anchored, now dream. Again, blend until powdered.

Last step is to add the rose petals and, as you blend again, think about the incense brew illuminating the heart and new moon visioning.

When milled down to your desired level, place into a clean sterile jar and store ready for your new moon divination.

Remember, we've assumed you have set your focus and intent, taken your safety into account, and are preparing your incense in an aerated space. This recipe gives you a powdery blend that is perfect for placing onto hot charcoal set in a heat proof dish. You only need the smallest amount (½ teaspoon) per ritual, placed onto the hot coal to set the space for your new moon magic.

Herb: Passionflower (Passiflora incarnata)
Moon: Half moon
Earth: Intention/harvest
Essence: Flow/potential

As we shift into the earth cycle of groundedness, intention and future harvest to move from the potency of the new moon to the waxing half moon, how can we divine for opening to potential in our magical work and castings? Welcome, passionflower.

The herb passionflower jumped out at me (literally said "Me!") as I walked through my garden contemplating the earth cycle and moon stages. This humble, subtle herb really can show what it means to be in a relaxed state whilst divining. It supports us into presence, into the now of the moment.

Passionflower is the herb of relaxation and restoration, one of the best ways to begin a divinatory journey. A nervine tonic, this herb supports journeying and will help you to repair and renew along the way. A relaxed nervous system can be one of the biggest supports when accessing all our realms and passionflower gets us there. Its deep green leaves speak of a richness in nutrients, its vines making their way on the path of least resistance with the smallest of tendrils reaching out and settling the host into a receptive state.

Monograph
Common Names: Passionflower
Latin Name: *Passiflora incarnata*
Plant Family: Passifloracea
Parts Used: Leaves, tendrils, and flowers
Botany: Climbing or prostrate vines with grasping tendrils. The plants can be herbaceous or woody. The simple leaves are entire or lobed, and a single plant may produce a diversity of leaf shapes. The flower sits on the vine sharing a divine sacred geometrical offering.
Harvest: Harvest the aerial parts of the plant and dry in a cool well-ventilated space. Your dried passionflower herb is best run through a 10 mm screen to complete the produced herb. Flowers are a welcome addition though will need to be harvested separately and dried for longer.
Active Constituents: Chrysin, vitexin, coumerin, and umbelliferone
Contraindications: Recommended to avoid during pregnancy.

Makings - divination body oil
This herb makes a fantastic divination body oil. Take ¼ cup of harvested dried herb, add to 1.5 cups of your favourite body oil (I use apricot kernel or fractionated coconut oil) and place in your blender. Blend on low for around 30-45 minutes. (You're aiming to get a little warmth in the brew. I don't use a thermometer – I use feel. I like to feel it as a warm cup of tea.) After your brew is complete, place in a sterilised jar and pop on your windowsill or in a sunny spot for two weeks, shaking daily. Your focus is present as you shake – you are making passionflower divination oil blend. At the end of two weeks, strain the blend through a muslin cloth (or a new washcloth) into your clean oil bottle and place into your ritual box. This little champion oil will be ready to accompany you on your journey.

I use the divination body oil to prepare for a divining ritual, usually alongside my Tarot. You choose how you use the oil. You are bringing the passionflower magic to your practice. With passionflower, I look towards a deeply relaxed state before rituals where I am setting goals and casting forward.

Don't forget to add your experiences to your Book of Shadows too. After you've used the passionflower divination body oil, journal or write how you feel and how this has worked for you. Write down your dreaming and experiences. If you're using this oil alongside Tarot, note the cards, their positioning and use it as an opportunity to reflect upon later.

Herb: Rose
Moon: Full moon
Earth: Harvest/gratitude
Essence: Hold/embody

And here we are harvesting our hard-earned abundance. It's the full moon. There is a reckoning in this phase of gratitude. All the effort and work that we've put in is now ready for harvest. This is blended with a moment of holding and embodying as we then prepare to release and surrender.

When I journeyed with rose, the shadow and light of this plant medicine literally sat me up. The words 'gratitude' and 'release' came to mind. As magic would have it, I was coming across passages in books and online readings telling me 'if you want the rose, you take the thorns' and it's at this stage of our magic making and divination where this plant and its offerings humbly sits. The dark and light. The deeply grounded tap root that holds the plant so firmly into the ground, supporting the layered leaves that look fierce yet are so gentle, the sharpest of thorns and, of course, the most sincerely delightful of aromas, taste, vision, and hope that is the flower.

Welcome to rose.

Monograph
Common names: Rose, dog rose, rose hip – for this making we are using the common rose. Don't let that stop you from investigating, tasting, smelling, and listening to all the others! Their nuances are divine.
Latin Name: *Rosa canina, Rosa rugosa, Rosa virginiana, Rosa canina, Rosa multiflora, Rosa damascena, Rosa gallica, Rosa centifolia, R. spinosissima* and the list goes on!
Plant family: Rosaceae
Parts used: Flowers
Botany: Many Roses are dense shrubs but some have vining habits; sometimes thorny, sometimes bristly stems, alternative pinnately compound leaf

structure with five to nine toothed leaflets; flowers radially symmetrical, colours ranging from white to red depending on species; sometimes fleshy hips orangey-red and crowned with five erect sepals often forming a five-pointed star shape. Inside the hip are many seeds attached to hairs.
Energetics: Heart medicine, aromatic nervine
Active Constituents: Geraniol, citronellol, nerol and linalool
Contraindications: None.

Makings – rose and fire

I love this blend and was led to share a ritual with you which is a regular at my home and hearth. The process of using the whole plant really sings. It's a great one to take bush too and you can make the base tea alongside fireside divination. It can also be added to so many aspects of your following day, bringing the energy of your ritual working with you.

You'll need an open fire, a billy (or saucepan), pure rainwater and a stick. I don't get into too many complexities in my divination magic (except black salt making but that is another story for another day) and this rose and fire energy brings simplicity, heart and grounding to your working. The simple act of making a fireside rose decoction will divine along the themes of gratitude and release. It opens the heart to listening and receiving.

Take approximately ¼ cup of dried organic rose petals and place into your fireside billy. Heat them ever so gently, releasing the rose aroma – only for about 30 seconds. You want to just begin to smell the aroma on offer as the plant's cell walls begin to break down. Slowly, mindfully add the rainwater. With focus and intent bring to a simmer, stirring deosil (clockwise). This is important. As the brew reaches a simmer, move to the side of the fire, and place the billy onto the coals. Listen to your thoughts, any conversations, bird calls, animals visiting, or whatever else is happening while brewing. This energy is all going into the fireside magic of the rose.

As the brew is cooling, prepare and strain into your clean bottle and keep the leftover matter, this will have an offering, a final statement to share with you. So, we've strained the rose water from the petals, bottled it and put it aside to drink the magic of our divining and intention. Now take the petals and spread them onto a large wooden board. Allow these to dry overnight by the campfire. See what they have to say in the morning. My petals often come up with a shape or symbol as a final message from the plant working. After reading, be sure to offer the rose petals back to the earth via your compost or garden. In the city? Gift rose to a tree in the local park.

This rose brew will last in the fridge for a week and can be used across the full moon in many ways. Drink it in small amounts, add it to a cacao brew, maybe a body scrub or bath salt is calling you. Pour it through your hair as a rinse and carry her magic with you all day.

As we move from the full moon energy of heart and gratitude into release and surrender, pour the decoction onto the earth to release. Back to the earth. The magic is done. Done.

Seed to Soul
Remember the full cycle of seed to soul as we work with plant and matter. We return the spent matter – whether it be ash from the mugwort smudge, the leftover leaves from a brewed dream state tea, or the dream pillow's content – back to the compost with reverence.

Our magic may begin when we open the circle or decide to pull out our Tarot or tea but it does not end there.

Anywhere you dispose of your spent matter is okay, as long as it's done with a sense of gratitude, reverence and (hopefully) joy for the divination completed and message received.

It is the closing of the cycle.

It is the practice.

The companies below have been chosen as they support Australian farmers. Their businesses prioritise regenerative farming practices and articulate where wildcrafted herbs are sourced. Great for magic makers as we aim for making from Seed to Soul.

- www.theherbcottage.com.au – live plants and dried herbs located in the Gold Coast hinterland, QLD.
- www.happyherbs.com.au – dried herbs and blends located in Newtown, NSW.

About Ki-ian

Ki-ian is an earth lover, herbalist and practitioner of embodied witchcraft who has her feet firmly planted in the soil. She contributed 'A Witch's Apothecary' chapter to Living Witchery Beginner Witch Guide *(published 2021)*

Spending her childhood weaving between her family home in the suburban outskirts of Sydney and the east coast bushlands, it was here Ki-ian's first learnt to sit in stillness listening to the cadence of nature observing her rhythm and flow.

In her on-farm apothecary she creates products deeply grounded in ritual with mindfully grown herbs, harvested to meet the needs of the magic. This manifests in the form of practical magic where essential oils, herbs and hydrosols are brewed into offerings that offer awakening to pleasure and purpose.

Ki-ian facilitates workshops and invites 1:1 internships where she teaches all aspects of matter to magic with a focus on regeneration, earth care and connection to country from which the matter is harvested.

For more information, visit solumfarm.com

Ogham – Divinatory Language of Plants

By Sandra Greenhalgh

Divination with Ogham ('oh-am') is a wonderful method which connects you deeply with trees and plants. Ogham is sometimes known as the 'Celtic tree alphabet'. It first appeared on stone monuments in Ireland, England, Scotland, Wales, and the Isle of Man around the 4th century. Ogham symbols were chiselled across the sharp edges of the stones, designed to be read vertically from bottom to top. Usually the inscriptions recorded people's names, marked boundaries, or declared land ownership. Ogham was later documented in manuscripts from the 6th to 9th centuries, written from left to right.

In addition to these prosaic uses of Ogham, there are also accounts of Ogham being written onto sticks to send secret messages, and used for magic.

Ogham is not the same as runes. Ogham links to Celtic lore.

Scholars (and I confess to not being a scholar or academic in this field) are not in consistent agreement regarding the origin of Ogham, nor do they agree as to how or why it was created. While Ogham script was used to write Old Irish, Old Welsh, Pictish, or Latin languages and it is believed to have been modelled on Greek, Roman, or runic characters, no source has been conclusively determined.

So let us turn to The Ogham Tract from the *Auraicept na N-Éces* ('*The Scholars Primer*') which provides us with a mythical explanation:

> *Now Ogma, a man well skilled in speech and in poetry, invented the Ogham. The cause of its invention, as a proof of his ingenuity, and that this speech should belong to the learned apart, to the exclusion of rustics and herdsmen...*

Whence is the origin of the Ogham? Not hard. I shall speak firstly of the woods of the trees whence names have been put for the Ogham letters…it is from the trees of the forest that names were given to the Ogham letters metaphorically.

The first Ogham script originally only included 20 letters, arranged into four groups (*'aicme'*, singular is *'aicmí'*) of five letters. Each letter consists of one to five straight lines, radiating out in different directions from the 'spine' or centre line. Later, five additional letters (extended vowels) were added, creating a fifth group – the *forfeda* or 'extra letters'. Each of these five groups is named after its first letter.

- The B aicme includes B, L, V/F, S, N and has lines to the right (or bottom if horizontal) of the spine.
- The H aicme includes H, D, T, C, Q and has lines to the left (or top if horizontal) of the spine.
- The M aicme includes M, G, NG, ST, R and has diagonal lines across the centre line.
- The A aicme includes A, O, U, E, I and has short lines perpendicular to both sides of the spine.
- The forfeda includes EA, OI, UI, IO, EA, a variety of different symbols radiating from the centre line.

Before we knuckle down into some divination methods using the Ogham, it's important to understand there are a myriad of different Ogham systems available. While key source material include the 12th century Irish *Book of Leinster*, the 14th century Irish *Book of Ballymote* (*In Lebor Oghaim*), and *The Scholars Primer*, interpretations and translations of the materials vary significantly. Ogham systems themselves have changed over time, which adds to the complexities.

My favourite system was popularised by Robert Graves in the book *The White Goddess*, published in 1948. Graves aligns Ogham symbols with trees, plants and – now somewhat controversially – a lunar calendar. Unfortunately, Grave's poetic interpretations, which incorporate O'Flaherty's *Ogygia* concepts, have since been slammed by academics for their many inaccuracies. Just as unfortunately, scholars don't necessarily agree with each other as to a 'one true Ogham' which makes historical accuracy and interpretations even more difficult.

Each Ogham letter has a name (or multiple names) and meanings, and that's where things start to get interesting, as Ogham script is intrinsically associated with trees and plants. There's a hidden realm of meaning within the Ogham. It's an ecosystem of connections which flow between history, the natural world, folklore, language, craftmanship, and Celtic cultures.

Imagine yourself walking through a forest, holding this book. Look at the trees and shrubs around you. See how the twigs connect to the branches which in turn connect to the trunk. Notice how they may overlap with those of other trees. Can you see the Ogham shapes within your surroundings? Not only can you observe the shapes of Ogham in these natural surroundings, the trees themselves are also keys to a myriad of mysteries. By walking in a forest – or a park – you are literally journeying within a living encyclopedia of tree wisdom and knowledge.

This tree wisdom and associated lore can be successfully tapped into through a range of divination methods. Below is a simple table that provides a snapshot of Ogham symbols, names, and divination meanings. It was developed from a range of information sources (including Liz and Colin Murray's *Celtic Tree Oracle*) as well as my own peculiarities. Unfortunately, it's beyond the scope of this chapter to include detailed information for each of the Ogham symbols, though suggestions for further study are included in the reference section if you'd like to dig deeper.

Ogham	Letter	Name	Gaelic names	Meanings
	B	Birch	Beith/Beithe	Beginnings, birth, new opportunities. Can signify a warning.
	L	Rowan	Luis/Lish	You are being protected from harmful influences. Listen to the flame of inspiration.
	F	Alder	Fearn/Fern	Inner faith, shield, foundation. Time for a sacrifice. Guardian.
	S	Willow	Saille/Sail	The unconscious, female, emotions, dreams, visions, healing, lunar cycles.
	N	Ash	Nuin/Nion/Nin	Strength, control, self-determination. Weaving. Spear. World tree.

Ogham	Letter	Name	Gaelic names	Meanings
	H	Hawthorn	Huathe/Uath	Wilderness, sexuality, cleansing. Contact with the Fae.
	D	Oak	Duir/Dair	Inner strength, endurance, doorway.
	T	Holly	Tinne	Time to be assertive, or for strong, bold actions.
	C	Hazel	Coll	Wisdom, divination, flow. Magic and poetry.
	Q	Apple	Quert/Cert	Abundance, beauty, generosity, otherworlds.
	M	Vine or Bramble	Muin	Teaching, exploration, truth, intoxication. Connection.
	G	Ivy	Gort	Gateways, movement, change and transformation.
	Ng	Broom or Reed	nGéadal/Getal	Communication, memory, healing.
	Ss/St	Blackthorn	Straif/Straiph	Challenges, foes, serious magic.
	R	Elder	Ruis	Renewal. Maturity that comes with experience.
	A	Fir or Pine	Ailim/Ailm	Objectivity, far seeing, marvelling.
	O	Gorse	Ohn/Onn	Harvest, fulfilment, passion.
	H	Heather	Úr	Good luck, loyalty.
	E	Aspen / White poplar	Eadha/Eadhadh	Truth, inner wisdom, communication with ancestors.
	I	Yew	Ioho/Idhadh	Ancestors, fate, continuity. Service. Regeneration.
	EA / CH	Aspen / Grove	Koad	A sacred place. Spiritual growth.

Ogham	Letter	Name	Gaelic names	Meanings
	OI/TH	Spindle / Ivy	Oir	Sweetness and joy. Gold. Honour. Vitality.
	UI/PE	Honeysuckle	Uillead/ Uillean	Hidden secrets.
	IO/PH	Gooseberry or Beech.	Iphin	Ancient knowledge. Sweetness, juiciness.
	CH/XI /AE	The sea / Beech	Mor	Travel. Hidden knowledge.

Ogham in your local (non-British Isles) biosphere

What are we to do when we don't live in a country with all the trees or plants listed above? For example, where I live in Queensland, eucalyptus varieties are predominant and European oak trees can't successfully grow as it's too warm. Half an hour's drive gets me to beautiful and lush rainforest environs and, of course, none of those plants are listed in the Ogham correspondences.

Fortunately, there are a few options available. For most of my straightforward divination work, I simply use the British Isles correspondences. I'm fortunate to have spent time getting to know the plants in those localities and have studied them extensively through Druidry. For divination castings, I use a set of handcrafted Ogham discs which were created from the dead branch of an Australian ironbark tree (*Eucalyptus sideroxylon*). Alternatively, I use the Murray's *Celtic Tree Oracle* card deck. But of course, this is not the only way to engage with the Ogham as a divination system if you don't live in the British Isles. There are some excellent alternatives, though some require quite a lot of time and focus.

Begin by doing an internet search to check if someone else has created a list of your local plant alternatives. For example, when I type in 'Australian Ogham' there's some nifty suggestions which appear on the screen in front of me. Other people have put in the effort and developed what they feel are appropriate 'swaps' for the western European trees and shrubs.

However, there are issues with this option, as native flora and fauna can differ dramatically between states and climates, even in the same continent or country. In addition, your lived experiences and knowledge may vary significantly from other peoples' findings. It can be a case of: "Why the heck does that person believe that banksia is the same as gorse?" Ogham correspondences just don't necessarily match up that smoothly in other countries.

Personally, I dislike the concept of directly swapping or ascribing non-European plants to the original Ogham tree correspondences. Many years ago, I tried to do this with local Australian trees, and it didn't easily or seamlessly work for me (or the trees!) due to the different landscape and stories. For example, while there are commonalities between the growth patterns of yew trees and Moreton Bay fig trees, you don't usually find Moreton Bay fig trees planted in cemeteries. Instead, maybe arctic beech trees share more in common with yew trees, as they live so long? Perhaps you can pop in macadamia trees for coll (hazel) as they both have nuts, but what of the different stories and myths associated with each of these trees?

This brings us to another option, which is to create a unique and personalised form of divination by engaging with your local plants and trees. The following techniques can also be used to create your local Ogham correspondences or develop your own system – or to receive direct divinatory messages from plants.

How to communicate with trees and plants
Chose to spend time with a particular type of plant (to avoid repetition I will just use the word plant, to include trees). Perhaps you have one growing in a pot, beside a footpath, in a park or nearby bushland. Consider the physical features such as leaf, flower, fruit shape, and the appearance of the bark.

Research the botanical name, and features of the plant. Does it have healing properties? Is it poisonous to certain creatures? What are the preferred conditions and where else does it grow? What are its germination needs and life cycles?

Respectfully learn about First Nations peoples' stories or myths associated with the plant.

Burn dry, discarded leaves, bark, or wood. If safe, smell the smoke. Watch how it burns, swiftly or slowly? Does it leave a pattern or residue?

Meditate with the plant to communicate and learn other mysteries, which may not be documented in the mundane world. This technique may involve receiving messages of 'unverified personal gnosis', i.e., significant to you, though not necessarily true for other people or circumstances. Here's some other suggestions to help you connect with plants:

- Take a journal with you to jot down thoughts and messages.
- Stand a short distance away from the plant. Enter a light, relaxed trance-like state where you feel free of anxiety or mundane thoughts. You can do this by breathing deeply and deliberately, releasing any

tension or stress from your body. Visualising roots flowing from the soles of your feet into the ground is a simple way to feel grounded.

✦ Looking at the plant, open your fingers with palms facing towards the plant. Quietly, slowly, and respectfully seek connection with the spirit/life energy/soul of the plant. Ask, aloud or silently, for the plant's permission to approach it and communicate. Wait patiently until you experience a feeling that the plant is willing or agreeable.

✦ If the plant doesn't want to talk to you, gently disengage. You may like to try again during another season or moon cycle, when the plant may be more receptive. On the other hand, there are trees and plants which almost leap into your path (or throw down a branch), as they want to connect with you. I've found there are social trees who love people. They are often located near parks or bends of walking tracks. Have you seen those trees with low, horizontal branches which have children climbing all over them? Those tree are often lively and love to engage.

✦ Don't rush things. Make sure you allocate enough time to undertake the connection process. Some plants (particularly ancient trees) take a long time before they notice you. After all, your lifetime to a centuries-old tree is like that of a dog's life cycle compared to a human.

✦ Once you get a feeling that the plant is agreeable to communicating with you – and this is a form a practical psychism – approach the plant. It may feel right to sit with your back against the trunk or hug the tree. Be guided by your intuition and the plant's responses.

✦ You may like to ask questions, or simply be receptive to the story of the plant, in the manner they wish to share it with you.

✦ When you have finished your plant communications, provide an offering. Never leave plastics (including synthetic fabric, thread, or ribbon) or non-compostables such as tealight cannisters! An offering can be as simple as a sharing some water, a song or poem.

You will find more information on plant communication in Ki-ian's chapter.

Creating your own Ogham set for divination
Ideally, an Ogham set is formed from wood or plant matter (even cardboard) though that's down to personal preference. Some people prefer to use stones, shells, clay or glass for their Ogham set, and those materials work just as well.

Before creating an Ogham set, you may like to ask aloud for the agreement and assistance of Ogma the Sun-Faced. He is recognised as an Irish god (or warrior) of the Tuatha Dé Danann.

Ogma, skilled in speech and poetry,
I ask for your blessings and guidance, as I create this set of Ogham,
Wrought from the natural world.
May these Ogham be imbued with mystery and honesty.
A channel from the otherworlds to now,
Accurate and uncanny in form.
May they speak truly.

The most common way to make an Ogham set for divination is to cut lengths of wood about 7-20 cm long and 1-5 cm thick, and then mark/carve the symbols onto the sticks. Carve a point at one end of the stave, or notch them to identify which end is up or down. The staves can then be protected with a coating of natural wax, oil, or varnish. You may like to only have 20 in your set, or 25 by including the extra five Ogham symbols of the Forfeda.

It's a magical process to create Ogham made from the wood of the actual tree itself, but that's not possible (or preferable) in all circumstances. Including wood from each corresponding tree is a consciously slow and deliberate act which can deepen your otherworldly connections with plant allies.

There are other ways to create a set of Ogham for divination. I love my set of ironbark Ogham discs. The symbols have been burnt into the wood, so I can feel them with my fingers, but painting or carving symbols works just as well. These discs can put up with a lot of knocking about, unlike staves which can be quite fragile, particularly if not stored carefully.

As Miranda also suggests in the rune chapter, you should create a home to safely store your Ogham set. Some people name the container which stores Ogham sets a 'crane bag', linking to an old Celtic verse found in *The Book of the Lays of Finn*:

The shirt of Manannan and his knife,
and Goibhne's girdle, altogether:
a smith's hook from the fierce man:
were treasures that the Crane-bag held.

The King of Scotland's shears full sure,
and the King of Lochlainn's helmet,
these were in it to be told of,
and the bones of Asal's swine.

Casting the Ogham

There are a variety of ways to use your Ogham set for divination. The simplest way is to intuitively choose one Ogham from your crane bag, and then ponder the associated meanings. You could do this once a day, or at certain times of the week/month/year, or to receive guidance when you have a question.

Other options are casting (gently throwing) the Ogham pieces onto the ground or 'mat' (of wood, cloth, or paper). You may choose to cast all Ogham pieces, or just some of them. Carefully review the predominant Ogham, the relationships between their positions and location on the mat. You can make your own sectioned mat by drawing three concentric circles, and ascribing the following meanings to Ogham falling in the different sections:

+ *Centre section* – the current situation or immediate focus
+ *Middle section* – future possibilities or desires
+ *Outer section* – unseen influences or the bigger picture.

Using Fionn's window as a casting mat is another way to perform divination with Ogham. Fionn's window (also called Fionn's shield) is named after the Irish hero, Druid, and chieftain, Fionn Mac Cumhaill. This design was documented in the 14th century *Book of Ballymote*, displaying Ogham letters in concentric circles rather than across a straight line. Some people believe that Fionn's window is a symbolic map of Celtic cosmology, and it certainly can be used as a mandala for reflection and contemplation. To perform divination using Fionn's window, simply cast one (or more) stones or tokens upon it, then reflect on the Ogham letters under or close by the token/s.

Connecting directly with plant and tree allies

Instead of making (or using) an Ogham set, you may wish to take a different approach by working directly and intuitively with the wisdom of the trees and plants. Try being guided by the natural world itself by entering a receptive state while outdoors. Sit still for a while, with your eyes closed.

When ready, open your eyes, and let your senses gently be drawn to a particular plant, leaf, twig, or flower, and be open to its message for you. Or, when walking, randomly stop in a certain place, spin around three times and then notice any patterns or unusual occurrences. It's not uncommon to have a leaf suddenly float down in front of you, or see a most wonderful fallen branch during these activities.

Regardless of how you prefer to work with the Ogham, it's a remarkable, insightful, and multifaceted divination method and well worth the effort to learn.

About Sandra Greenhalgh

Sandra is an author, artist and occultist who lives in Brisbane, Australia. A long-term participant, student, and teacher of Western Mystery traditions, she joined The Order of Bards, Ovates and Druids in 1988, while working in England.

Growing up in the Queensland countryside helped foster her deep love of the wild places of bush, beach, and the outback. Whenever possible, Sandra retreats to camping beside the ocean with her extended family and friends.

Sandra has over 30 years of Neopagan community involvement. Tarot and divination are passions, and in 2019 Sandra created a new deck of oracle cards focussing on Druidic lore, called the Druid Wisdom Oracle. *She also authored the* Druid Wisdom Oracle Guidebook, *released in 2020.*

In 2020, Sandra co-edited and contributed to A History of Druidry in Australia, *which includes contributions from over 30 Australians who practise Druidry. She is author and co-editor of* Living Witchery: Beginner Witch Guide *(released 2021).*

Sandra is grateful to live with her husband, two grown children and a couple of spoilt cats. Between writing, drawing, and procrastinating, she works in healthcare.

See byrningtyger.com *for more information.*

FOUNDATIONS: Traditional Forms

These forms of divination usually require a higher level of skill and technical interpretation in comparison to simpler folk-magic forms of divination. Some have historical origins which are over a thousand years old.

Divining With Horary Astrology

By Kim Fairminer

Some astrologers argue that astrology is not or should not be divinatory. However, that perspective severs astrology from its innately divine source – the stars themselves.

The stars, including the Sun at the centre of our solar system, offer light, warmth, and life. For eons, this radiance has been associated with spirit, the animating life-giving spark in the mysterious limitless void of dark space. There are cultures throughout human history who revered the Sun itself as a deity.

It makes sense to look to the stars to see the Will of the Divine. Humans have been honing interpretive astrological techniques for thousands of years. We'd be missing out on a great swathe of ancestral cultural wisdom if we were to disregard astrology's divinatory potential.

While you can use many predictive techniques perfected by ancient and modern practitioners of the art of astrology, horary astrology is the most divinatory technique.

Horary astrology is intricate. You cannot master it overnight. It requires dedicated study to learn and years of practice before you become even half good. But by pulling back the curtain a little here, I hope I can entice your astrological curiosity away from natal charts and into the uncanny world of horary astrology.

What can you ask?

Divination starts with a question, a wondering… Is my love is reciprocated? Will I get the job? Will X pay me back the money? Am I going to jail?

Don't laugh. If you're in that situation, it's a genuine and pressing question, and one that I am asked often enough in my work as an online 'psychic'. Legal questions are common but mostly I am asked about love and money. One of my colleagues eloquently summed up 80% of client questions as being: "Am I getting laid? Am I getting paid?"

Did you notice that all these questions are closed and can be answered with either a 'yes' or a 'no'?

A horary chart will certainly flesh out the whys and the hows along the way, but horary's strength is honing in on the answer to 'will I?' (which we will work through shortly), the 'when?', and the 'where?'. The latter two questions are trickier skills to master, but the example chart later in this chapter demonstrates some simple timing concepts.

'Should' questions are to be avoided. Questions phrased in this way are asking for an opinion and the planets are disinterested. If you want an opinion, ask the Tarot. If you want an impartial answer from the stars, reword your question.

It helps to put a time frame on the question. "Will I begin a long-term romantic relationship this year?" is a lot more practical, grounded, and ethical (even if you are reading for yourself) than "Will I ever meet my soul mate?"

Personally, I use horary to find lost items, navigate career issues, choose courses of study, make investment decisions, and – much to the chagrin of my friends – decide whether I will attend public events.

Professionally, most of my horary work focuses on relationship matters, real estate negotiations, legal situations, and business/career questions.

Horary is super versatile and super practical.

Asking the question

The horary moment grabs you. A question can present itself like a lightbulb flicking on to tell you it is time to cast a chart. Sometimes, the world places obstacles between your horary moment and sitting down to cast the chart. In that case, you may like to note down the time of the 'lightbulb moment' for later. At other times, the opposite occurs, and a question lingers unasked. You try to put it out of your mind and/or deal with the situation in the material world, but it just won't resolve and eventually you cannot *not* cast the chart to see what is going on. Either way, the horary moment has a hold on you.

You need a certain mindset, mental and physical space, and spiritual spaciousness, to sit with the planets and listen to what they have to say. It's not a purely intuitive process. Horary (and astrology more broadly) requires your whole brain. Your intellect and your intuition need to dance. And when they do, you see beyond the curious numbers and symbols on the zodiacal wheel. You follow those fractals, you discern patterns, and you can see the Will of the Divine.

The chart is never wrong but the astrologer sometimes is. Perhaps we're too close to the situation and have a preferred outcome in mind and simply ignore what the chart is telling us. Just as often, the complexity of the situation is reflected in the nuances of the chart and the answer isn't always immediately apparent.

I relish a quick and obvious horary chart with all the subtlety of being hit by a four-by-two. When I get one of those, I feel like the Universe is giving me a high five. Sometimes we need that reassurance.

In a nutshell, horary is a chart cast at the moment the astrologer fully understands the question, whether they are asking for themselves or being asked by another person. Getting to the right question can be quite a process. It is worth spending time identifying what you most need to know in this exact moment.

I keep saying 'the moment'; it is *all* about the moment.

The Universe is a big place with many intricate nooks and crannies. It's helpful and time-efficient to be specific. What do you *really* want to know right now? The Gods are waiting to be asked.

> Don't ask nonsense questions.
> The Gods don't care what you choose for breakfast and it's none of your business if a celebrity had an affair.

Horary is different than seeing your astrologer for your year ahead forecast, which of course is a fabulous thing to do. But a 12-month window is open to many possibilities. Often in a year ahead forecast, there is something quite specific that the client really wants to know about. Something specific, like a promotion at work, an addition to the family, or an inheritance.

When we ask a question – a *significant* question – and care about the answer, whether we speak it out loud or only with our inner voice, who are we speaking to? Are we are speaking to God, the divine, the Universe, our inner self? However, you want to frame it, this entity we speak to is wisdom outside of our ordinary ourselves – all we need to do is stop and ask the question. That is divination.

> Be upfront with your diviner about what you really want to know.
> Ask a better question and you get a more accurate reading.

Answering the question / Delivering judgement

The question is asked, any necessary clarification occurs, and once confirmed, the astrologer casts a chart for that moment in their own location.

The astrologer is not an absent channel as they are intimately involved in the divinatory process. They can even be seen in the chart, in the 7th house. Sometimes the horary chart advises the astrologer to be extra cautious about the judgement.

Judgement. That's a weighty word, isn't it?

The astrologer judges the chart and gives a specific answer to the question. It may be 'yes'; it may be 'no'; it may be a specific timeframe.

There is no fudge factor here. The astrologer has skin in the game.

In the presence of the divine, we are reminded of our human condition – our frailties, our responsibilities, our blind spots. And of course, we're also reminded of our direct and embodied experience of the divine. The divine is in us and we are in the divine.

More practically, you'll need an extensive astrological vocabulary, chart software, reference books, and, ideally, lessons from an experienced horary astrologer. (I highly recommend the practitioner's course offered by the School of Traditional Astrology.) You will also need above-average tenacity to study the details held by the chart and the confidence to form a judgement.

Even then, you won't get it right every time. But once the event unfolds, you can check the chart and see that it happened exactly as the planets described. Another rarer but fabulous result is that the divinatory act itself activated the free will of the querent to change the most likely outcome.

Who's who / Identifying significators

Everything in the world can be seen in the chart. Your sister's boyfriend. The company's money. Your missing glasses. A troublesome neighbour. They're all there.

The first part of solving the horary mystery is identifying who's who in the chart. You can decide on your strategy before you even look at the chart. For example, if you are wondering about pregnancy, you are primarily interested in the 1st house and the 5th house.

The querent is always the 1st house and the planet that rules the 1st house.

The 'quesited' is what the querent wants (whether it's a person or a thing) and is identified through the relevant house and the planet that rules that house cusp.

This is where a rulership textbook comes in handy. My favourites are Deborah Houlding's *The Houses: Temples of the Sky* and Lee Lehman's *The Book of Rulerships*. For example, a pet is 6th house, your fiancé is 7th house, the government is 10th house. A missing object is signified by the 2nd house, its ruling planet, and the Moon. The 4th house will describe where it is.

Houses are important in horary astrology because they anchor your topic of enquiry to Earth. Like the meaning assigned to each card position in a cartomancy spread, houses are particular places that represent particular subjects.

The division of houses is directly connected to the location on Earth, by latitude and longitude. While it's open to personal astrological preference, most horary charts are cast in Regiomontanus, which is the house system used by 16th century astrological genius, William Lilley. The following table will help you get started with house rulerships of common topics.

House	Topics
1st	The querent. Life, vitality, health, physicality, appearance.
2nd	Assets, money, resources, income, cash flow, wealth.
3rd	Siblings, cousins, neighbours, short journeys, communication.
4th	Home, family, parents, ancestry, the land.
5th	Children, pregnancy, sex, romance, pleasure, leisure.
6th	Illness, employees, daily routines, domestic chores, pets.
7th	Relationships, marriage, business partners, adversaries.
8th	Finance, debt, inheritance. Death, fear, anxiety.
9th	Overseas travel, foreigners, lawyers, spiritual practices, university.
10th	Career, status, fame, public roles, reputation, success.
11th	Friends, supporters, networks, luck, optimism.
12th	Secrets, unknown enemies, jail, hospital, self-undoing.

Essentially, what you are doing here is filtering out the planetary symbols to only those relevant to the question. You need to know who your querent is in the chart and which planet is the quesited.

After identifying the relevant house, look to the planet that rules the sign on the cusp of the house. Stick with traditional planetary rulerships, even if you use the modern rulership scheme for natal charts. If you have a Pisces rising chart, your querent is Jupiter, not Neptune. Scorpio is ruled by Mars (not Pluto) and Aquarius is ruled by Saturn (not Uranus).

Once you know who is who, you can move on to finding out what they're up to. The houses and the planet that rules the sign on the house cusp are of critical importance when answering horary questions. While Venus, for example, is a natural signifier of relationships, the planet that rules the descendant (7th house) of the horary chart will offer more important and specific information about the partner in question.

A planet within the house you are interested in is also significant. If Saturn is in the 7th house, the astrologer might mess up in some way or be unappreciated by the client (which is always of interest to me).

First impressions
Look at the ascendant. If a very early degree is rising, this suggests that the question is 'undercooked.' It is likely too soon to ask the question and more time must pass or more information is required. A very late degree rising says that the situation is about the change and the question may be redundant or 'overcooked'. Perhaps the querent knows more than they claim?

Pay attention to planets on the angles (that is conjunct the ascendant, midheaven, descendant, or imun coeli) as they make a major statement about the overall situation. Benefics on the angles are a good omen. Jupiter or the Sun on the midheaven are testimony that the truth will come to light. Malefics indicate trouble. Mars on the ascendant is a good indication that your querent is angry and/or impatient. Neptune rising suggests the querent is confused, absent-minded, or maybe even under the influence.

As the fastest moving of all the planets, the Moon is of critical importance to the horary chart. The Moon shows the flow of events. Depending on the question, it acts as co-significator for the querent or, if you're asking about an object, it signifies the movement of that object.

Describing the players
The sign on the cusp of a house and the ruling planet will help you describe the person or thing. You can extract quite specific information about a person's physical appearance and their psychological state by delving into description based on the element, modality, temperament, planet etc.

For example, a Saturnian person is likely to be mature, serious, and stick to the rules. A Mercurial person will have a long thin nose, be intelligent and communicative, and influenced by those around them.

Whether the person uses these qualities for good or ill can be assessed through planetary dignity. An essentially dignified planet lives up to the best of its abilities; an essentially debilitated planet generally exhibits the negative qualities of the planet. The Saturnian person becomes depressed, the Mercurial person gossips and steals.

This also works with the quesited, which may be an object rather than a person.

If you were answering a question about a dog and it was signified by Venus in Pisces, you'd know that it was a well-mannered and aesthetically pleasing animal with no shortage of friends and admirers. If you were asking about a job signified by Jupiter in Virgo, you'd assume it was a respected position involving teaching or mentoring but also a lot of hard work.

What's happening / Aspects

It's good to be able to confirm the identity of planetary players by describing the qualities of the person that planet represents and confirm their past actions with your client. That's how you know you've got the right person/planet and you're on the right track with your interpretation.

Once you've identified who's who and got a feel for who they are and what they're up to, double-check what they've already done by looking at the separating aspects (planets moving away from each other). Looking back helps confirm you have identified the parties correctly and builds your confidence in the chart. If your querent signified by Mercury is separating from a square to Mars, this could point to a recent argument, accident, or injury.

Applying aspects (planets coming together) tell you what is going to happen and are the key to accurate prediction. This is possible because the movement of planets is measured and predictable.

A planet changing signs can show someone going from a difficult situation to a more positive one, if the planet gains dignity in the new sign. This also works the other way. If a planet moves from a sign where it is happy into a sign where it is less able to express its natural disposition, the person or thing represented by this planet can expect to meet with challenges.

One planet forming an aspect to another planet indicates interaction between the people represented by those planets. This is particularly important for relationship queries. Usually, with matters of the heart, you want to see the significators of each person coming together in fortuitous circumstances and be able to deliver good news to your client. Sometimes you see separating aspects instead.

A trine brings ease and agreements; if the trine is separating, the parties decide on an amicable separation. An opposition can suggest an argument or a dramatic separation – a Full Moon occurs when the Moon is opposite the Sun so that gives you some sense of the energy – like a rubber band being stretched until it snaps. A square tends to indicate entrenched tension and hostility. Applying squares and oppositions bring people together but it's unlikely be what you hoped for or worth the effort involved.

A planet coming out from under the beams of the Sun (a conjunction) suggests the themes of that planet are returning to visibility, much like a New Moon. And just like a New Moon, this planet is likely to carry a death/rebirth story.

The direction and pace of the planets vary. Check if the planet is retrograde. A slow planet indicates a slow-moving situation; likewise, fast-moving planets expedite things. A retrograde planet means things are under review and not moving forward as expected.

The degrees between aspects are important. Which planet is moving faster? Has the aspect already perfected? Does another planet come along first to interrupt proceedings? This is where horary becomes intricate. Although not always relevant to the question, the number of degrees before or after an aspect helps with timing – which works backwards into the past, and forwards into the future.

Example chart: will the loan settle today?
Here's an elegantly simple horary chart. The client was anxious to receive confirmation that the refinancing of his home loan had settled as planned.

Which houses would we look at to answer this question? Mostly this question is about exchanging money so we'd look to the 2nd (querent's money) and the 8th house (debt, loans). We would also look at the 1st house to find out about the querent and perhaps the 4th house for the property.

I always look at the rising sign first. It's in the early degrees of Taurus. Given the question was asked before close of business on settlement day, the client's question was premature. Taurus also rules the 2nd house cusp, which described the querent's money. Taurus offers the stability of fixed Earth, so this is a good indication that the scheduled financial exchange will be fulfilled as planned.

Then I tend to look at the Moon. In this chart, the Moon is applying to (approaching) Jupiter, which is well positioned in the 10th house. This is an excellent indication that the querent's desires will be fulfilled. Jupiter and the Moon are both in Aquarius, another fixed sign which helps 'lock in' the desired outcome. The flow of energy (Moon) is moving towards the benefic Jupiter, which rules Pisces on the 11th house cusp (the querent's hopes and dreams).

The querent's home is signified by Leo on the 4th house cusp (home, real estate). Leo's ruling planet is the Sun, and we see the Sun in the 8th house of debt and loans, perfectly descriptive of a mortgage.

While I don't always look at the nodes, they are relevant because they are in houses directly involved in the question. The nodes are on the 2nd/8th cusps and describe the situation. The north node brings increase to the house of the querent's money, while the south node reduces debt. By changing banks, the querent saves himself some money over the life of the loan.

Going back to the querent and the 1st house, the presence of Uranus describes the querent's sense of urgency and his (over)active mind. The ruling planet of Taurus is Venus. Venus is weakly placed in Capricorn, in the cadent 9th house, conjoined to Pluto. The querent isn't in a powerful position and can't do anything except wait. The querent (Venus) is at the whim of the bureaucratic machinations of lawyers and banks at the big end of town.

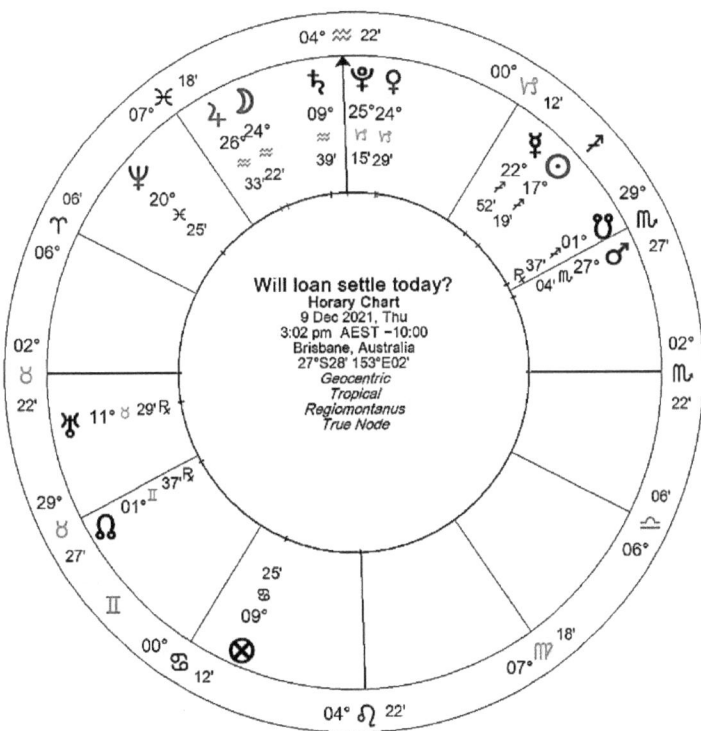

Above image produced in Solar Fire.

I advised my client to relax as the outcome was out of his hands, settlement would proceed according to established processes, and he would soon receive confirmation that the transaction was complete.

Regarding timing, the Moon is two degrees away from perfecting the conjunction to Jupiter and Mars is two degrees off the cusp of the 8th house. The chart was cast at 3:02 pm and, sure enough, settlement was confirmed two hours later at 5 pm.

But what about my free will?

A horary chart tells you what is most likely to happen in any given situation based on actions that have already occurred. It's like watching a ball roll down a hill. The ball will get to the bottom unless you use your free will and intervene to change the outcome.

A horary chart can show you where you are best placed to exercise your free will to influence the trajectory of events in your preferred direction. Sometimes there's not much you can do; other times you can call on the support of helpful planet/person to attain your desired outcome.

Just like the astrologer, the client/querent is intimately involved in the horary chart. Not a mere passive observer of fate unfolding.

If there was no possibility of change, no possibility of influencing the outcome, we wouldn't bother with divination. The existence of divination proves we have free will, the opportunity to engage with destiny and co-create an alternate outcome. Why else would we bother divining? If there wasn't an opening for your free will, there could be no divination. Of course, everyone else *also* has free will, which makes it tricky.

Divination is an engagement with the divine and we are part of that. We all have a role to play as active participants in the unfolding of the Universe.

This chapter is only a brief introduction to the wondrous art of horary astrology. If you are astrologically minded, I whole-heartedly encourage you to dive deeper into this fascinating and practical method of divination.

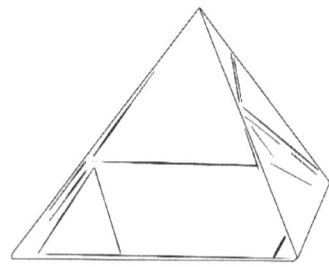

About Kim Fairminer

Kim is an astrologer, writer, and witch with more than 20 years hands-on experience as a magical practitioner. She has been a member of The Circle Coven for over ten years, including six years in the role of High Priestess. Before her life-changing midlife transits, she was an editor for a multinational company. She is author and co-editor of Living Witchery: Beginner Witch Guide *(published in 2021), writes horoscopes and forecasts for a range of publications, and shares esoteric wisdom in her online community. Kim writes, stargazes, and circle-casts from her home in suburban Brisbane.*

You can learn more about her work at kimfairminer.com

Scrying and Black Mirrors

By Lisa-jane Mason

> *"If you can look into the seeds of time, and say which grain will grow and which will not...."*
>
> Banquo speaks to the three witches, in Shakespeare's *Macbeth* (1606).

When I encounter the words divination and scrying, I imagine a seer, a medieval priestess with long flowing hair, wearing a Celtic fashioned robe, peering into a natural well in the forest. This image is probably influenced by my childhood fascination with the priestesses of Avalon and Arthurian novels. My mind's eye also conjures up another, more popular image – the wicked queen in *Snow White* with her famous evocation, "Mirror, mirror on the wall, who is the fairest of them all?" In these projections, we have a romanticized image of scrying and then, the socially popularized evil and dark 'wicked witch'.

My journey with scrying began as a little girl in primary school. I was a child who spent much of her time reading, daydreaming and living mostly in my fantasy realms and only partly in the mundane. From these early beginnings, my interest in the occult, witchcraft, and magick has persisted throughout most of my life. At 18, I began formal esoteric training when I joined my first coven. But it was a few years later, when I joined Nuit's Veil, that the realms of magick and transformation truly began to open to me and shift my reality.

Standing alone in a candlelit room, wearing a black robe, the sound of the priestess' shimmering bells alerted me that she was drawing closer to summon me. She took my hand and asked, "Are you ready?"

I was ready and it was that night I danced sky clad and raised the cone of power with my forever coven, my witchy family Nuit's Veil – Dark Circle. A few of us from Nuit's Veil – Dark Circle eventually went on to develop our own covens. I founded Babalon's Rising and joined the Ordo Templi Orientis.

Many of us still practice together, run events and initiations together, and visit each other's coven feasts and rites.

In the temple room of Nuit's Veil in St Peters, there hung a beautiful, large concave mirror above the altar. At times you would catch glimpses of the dancing witches reflected in the face of the magick mirror, and at other times it was as if other worldly beings would appear. The magick mirror is, for me, a tool that evokes mysterious intrigue but also a hint of fear and anxiety.

But what is scrying? According to Raymond Buckland in *Buckland's Complete Book of Witchcraft*, he describes scrying as a fascinating practice that enables the witch to 'literally see the future (or present or past)'. He states that just about any reflective surface can be used.

Historically, various claims have been made regaarding the kinds of communications that can be achieved through use of black mirrors. I have come across mentions of the black mirror being used to communicate with angelics, goetic demons, deceased ancestors, and even extra-terrestrial beings. The kinds of things communicated would vary from finding a missing object to revealing a dishonest lover, to past life information or universal mysteries and keys to great magical knowledge.

To be a seer, 'to be able to see', to have 'the sight', to have access to hidden information from the past, present, and future has held my curiosity for a very long time. One of my earliest memories of a successful magical experiment is from when I was in primary school.

My curiosity of all things esoteric had been sparked early in life. When I was about seven years old, I would gather my little friends together in the school playground at recess and lunch. We would hide at the edge of the playground amongst the trees and attempt all sorts of things, like séances, communing with the dead, and levitation.

One lunch time in grade five, my friends and I secretly gathered in the sports shed and closed the door. Someone produced a candle and a lighter and lit the candle. Someone else turned off the light.

In the dark candlelit shed, we began our plea with the elemental spirits, "If anyone is there, make the flame go out and come back on again… make the flame go out and come back on again…" We petitioned the spirits with intensity, separately and at times in unison, and then, suddenly, the flame flickered out and on again. Within an instant, there were dramatic loud shrieks and squeals. We all made a mad rush for the door, bursting into the safety of the sunlight and the school playground.

Here's an example of a simple candle scrying activity, based on an experience from my teens. One night, I was sitting at my small table in my van (painted with a huge black pentagram) and decided to try out scrying into a flame.

"Let me see, let me see what is to be." I called to the spirit of the flame before me. I repeated this chant many times for a long time. Eventually, I fell into a light trance. My gaze at the flame was soft and relaxed. I chanted until the words came out of my mouth without any thought required.

The flame began to twist and turn, burning bright and strong and moving in a rhythmic pattern. I continued to chant as the flame twisted and turned. It then appeared as a veiled woman. She continued her rhythmic dance, flickering back and forth. I felt excited but persisted with my mantra, my heart beating quickly and loudly, still holding my gaze, and continuing my spell.

Suddenly the cloak was removed to reveal a distinct image of a man's face with a short goatee beard. As quickly as he appeared he was then cloaked again. Simultaneously, as I gasped, the glass candle holder shattered!

My heart was racing.

I jumped into my bed grabbing the only book on witchcraft I had in my possession at the time and turned to *The Difference between Witchcraft and Satanism* chapter, which outlined that practicing witchcraft was safe and not evil, like Satanism was. I laugh about my naivety now.

I still recall that flame dancing, the veiled woman, and the bearded man as clearly today as when it happened many years ago. I have often wondered who that bearded man is, and why that was the image shown to me that night. I also wonder about the glass shattering. It was startling and terrifying. Maybe the glass container overheated? Maybe there was already a crack in it? I don't know. The timing was uncanny. Maybe it was magick.

Black mirrors

Elements in nature have historically been utilized to access information about our past, present, and future that is – for the most part – unknown. Witches are often drawn to scrying using water or fire as their tools. Other alternatives are conjuring entities into 'seeing stones' or 'magic mirrors' though these are outside the scope of this chapter. This leads us to the black mirror. In my experience in modern occult communities, this is a divination tool commonly used by witches.

Two of the most predominant occultists to use a black mirror for scrying are Edward Kelley and John Dee. They partnered up in the 1500s, and Edward Kelley is famous for offering his services as an advisor to Queen Elizabeth I. But what the pair are most well-known for is their ceremonial workings exploring what they referred to as a*ethyrs*. They also communicated with angels via their black mirror (which was known as a 'shew stone').

Through these communications, an entire language and magickal system known as Enochian was translated and formed. Occultists such as Aleister Crowley and modern-day practitioners such as Lon Milo DuQuette have delved into the world of Enochian practices. I've also studied Enochian magick, but that's a topic for another time.

The first time I used a black mirror, I was at my coven sister Kylie's house for a Plum Tree Grove coven meeting. Kylie and I had met a few years earlier in our parent coven, Nuit's Veil, and had become fast friends.

The witches had gathered. We were sitting around the table and had a variety of magical tools in front of us. All coven members were willing and eager to delve into the unknown and the magick of scrying. Some of us had glass balls, others had bowls filled with water with black ink added and I had scored one of Kylie's black mirrors.

The circle was cast, and Kylie's voice was powerful and enchanting as she cast the spell, moving the witches between worlds, opening the portal, and allowing us to tap into our extra senses. The aim was to have our past lives revealed to us.

I peered into the black mirror as I had learned and practiced over time. This technique includes using a soft and relaxed gaze with the focus somewhat beyond and deeper than the mirror's surface. Indistinguishable shapes formed and disappeared on the mirror. As more shapes appeared, they began to give way to scenery, and I could see vast land and mountains.

Then the mirror returned so that I could see the faded outline of my own face in the mirror's reflection. Slowly my features became clearer, but to my surprise, they were not my own – well, not of this lifetime and those I was familiar with. To shock me even further, the face whose features were becoming even more distinct appeared to be those of a man. A man!

I was horrified, for at that time in my life I had a lot of issues with the masculine and fancied that I would never have been such a lowly manifestation in a past life. I preferred the fantasies of princesses, priestesses, and forgotten royalty and expected, surely, that this is what would be revealed to me.

The first man's face then shifted into another man's face and again, another man! I cannot recall exactly how many were shown, but there was not one female face that appeared in the mirror that night. The last man's face shifted, to my surprise, changing into an image that was not even human, and quite alien.

This left me with quite a lot to ponder and I still reflect on it now. I wonder about those men's faces and my experience of men in this lifetime. I wonder if I was an awful male and my soul lesson in this lifetime is to be a woman at the hands of awful men. I know seeing the face that was not human was the first time that I contemplated the possibility of having come from the stars, other galaxies, and dimensions.

How to make a black mirror
What you need
- Black paint. Acrylic is fine.
- A picture frame. I like to find old vintage ones at charity shops.
- Herbs for divination, such as wormwood, sage, belladonna, datura (not for ingesting).
- Cauldron, or a saucepan if you don't have one.

Method
Preferably cut the herbs from your own witch's garden, or obtain from a coven sister or brother. If not, stores such as Happy High Herbs or online can provide you with fair quality herbs. I prefer ones I have grown myself and with magical intent as they definitely add that extra witchy whip.

Depending on the amount of herbs, choose the amount of water accordingly. Personally, I do not use measurements. I work on instinct. The last time I prepared this divinatory filter there were seven witches making mirrors, so the brew amount needed to be large. I had roughly a bucket of herbs and a good 10-litre pot. I used wormwood and sage from my garden and datura from an essence a witch friend had given to me.

Add the herbs to the cauldron, bring to boil, and then simmer for about three hours. As the brew is simmering and reducing, when you stir, be sure to add a chant, such as:

I/we stir this brew,
it's witch's dew,
to give me/us sight
upon this night.

Simmer until the brew is reduced to a very small amount, approximately 100 ml. Strain the herbs and leave them at your usual place for offerings.

Add very small amounts of the witch's dew into the black paint, approximately 2 mls. You don't want your paint to become too watery.

Remove the back piece from the vintage frame and paint the front part facing the glass. One coat will do, but three is better. Once again when painting, it's best to add a little chant, such as:

As I paint this black,
the veil drops back,
so that we may we see
what's to be (or what has been).

Allow to dry. Put the frame back together.

Consecration of the black mirror

This can be as simple as gathering the elements (Earth, Air, Fire, Water) and anointing your new magical tool with each element. You will need a chalice with water and a pentacle. In our coven, our pentacle is a wooden disk which has a five-pointed star (pentagram) on it. You could also use a pentagram amulet or trace a five-pointed star with your wand, index finger, a flame, a censor, or incense sticks.

We usually also anoint the black mirror with sabbath oil and ritual wine. This can be done during an elaborate rite. The practice of anointing is used to mark the tool as sacred and magical. Also, depending on the properties of the oil and wine used, these can heighten the particular type of magick you are intending. The important thing is that the new magical tool, the black mirror, is consecrated.

Some people may argue whether consecration is a necessary process. To be honest, I have used tools that have been consecrated and others that haven't been. Personally, I have found that if I take the time to consecrate and dedicate a tool to its purpose, it seems to work that little better and have a certain shine. Unconsecrated or consecrated, no ritual or elaborate ritual, it can all work depending on the witch's personal tastes and desires. Some of us are concise and practical, while others draw on, rely upon, and adore the more dramatic.

Using the black mirror

Unfortunately, for most of us, using a black mirror is not as simple as purchasing a mirror, casting a circle, reciting an incantation, and summoning visions. It all comes down to the individual, but it could take months before you develop the ability to see visions in fire, water, or mirrors.

Generally, developing the ability to scry relies on doing foundational activities to develop your third eye and induce altered states of consciousness.

This will eventually allow you to be able to utilize this extra witchy sense. It's important to practice meditation, and visualisation exercises.

When I started building my connection to my third eye, I would visualise a piece of fruit like an apple. I would focus on details such as the colours of the apple, seeing where it was shiny or dull. I would visualise a bite being taken out of it and pay attention to the juices dripping forth. If jumping straight to an apple is a little difficult, it's good to start with visualising colours. I like to visualise walking up a staircase, and each stair is a different colour – red, orange, yellow, green, blue, indigo, and violet. It's also nice to do a little meditation after this colour exercise.

Top tips
Considering the lessons learned in my early forays into scrying, here are my top tips:

- ✦ Cherish your tools and process.
- ✦ Centre and ground yourself before starting to scry.
- ✦ Safety first, particularly if you are scrying with fire.
- ✦ Be ready for your scrying session to work, yet come without expectations of what you will see.
- ✦ A mantra is a highly effective way to change consciousness.
- ✦ Gaze softly with your focus beyond and deeper than the mirror's surface.
- ✦ Practise, practise, practise.
- ✦ Journalling is important, as is sharing experiences with other witches. It's helpful to document the time, place, phase of the moon, where you were, methods used, and any desirable and undesirable outcomes.
- ✦ Experiment with different phases of the moon, times of the day and different times of the year.

Why
I think it's important to reflect on the 'why'. When setting out to learn a new practice, it's good to have some understanding of your own motivations. At times, it's an innate calling to an art and you just know it's for you. Some people may just be simply eager to experiment, to see if it works, a bit like a science project.

I hope this chapter has sparked an interest for you and provided you with enough information to get down to your local vintage shop, find a cool frame, and get crafting on your very own black mirror!

In Nomine Babalon!
777

About Lisa-jane Mason
Lisa-jane is a Thelemic, Mystic Witch living in the Northern Rivers NSW ('Rainbow Country'). Lisa-jane founded Babalons' Rising in 2009 and has run many esoteric workshops and retreats. A fan of psychodrama and ceremonial ritual, a working for the core coven usually takes at least six months to perfect. Lisa-jane is also a Kunadlini Reiki Master and now spends most of her time focused on healing and planning events for the Northern Rivers region.

Runes – Divination with Long Branches of the Younger Futhark

By Miranda Kopittke

Mythologically speaking, the runes are a physical manifestation from the divine, which act as a gateway for communication from metaphysical to the physical of our realities. They provide us with a way to understand the mysteries of life in its entirety. Working with them can affect our lives when used for spellcraft and they give us clarity when used for divination.

The runes were not created as such but rather they existed and were acquired by Odin during a nine-night vigil. In pursuit of wisdom, he swayed on the windswept tree of Yggdrasil. It was during this deep, ecstatic trance that the runes appeared to him, he took them up and in turn he gifted them to humanity.

While the symbols and staves were given to us by Odin, it was Heimdall (pronounced; hame-dahl) who taught humans rune knowledge. Heimdall is the guardian of Bifrost, the rainbow bridge and is credited as being the father of humanity through the formation of societal structures and human relationships. If you decide to pursue the runes in earnest, then I highly recommend developing a relationship with one of these runic deities.

Runes were in use across a large section of ancient Europe known in the old world as Germania. With the first official archaeological evidence appearing on a brooch dated to 50 AD. There has been much debate about the historic origin of the runes with some suggesting they evolved from an ancient version of a Mediterranean alphabet or a mix of several. However, solid primary evidence is lacking, and this theory is refuted as much as it is postulated.

The word 'rune' basically means mystery or secret, which is why it is sometimes used for other systems of divination such as witches runes or Celtic runes. If you are even slightly familiar with the runes, you may have noticed differences between sets and meanings and you might be feeling a little confused about which is the 'right' one. Chances are that all of them are correct for a particular time, language variation, phonetic spelling, or context.

We can describe the runes as having evolved from the common language across Scandinavia during the Viking era known as Dansk Tunga, the Danish tongue, which we now call Old Norse. This language had regional differences we could liken to today's English variants in England, America, and Australia.

Runic alphabets are named after the phonetic value of the first six runes, which is where we get futhark from. In the elder futhark this is Feoh, Úruz, Þurisaz, Ansuz, Raiðo and Kenaz. The adaptation of language from Proto-Indo-European into Old Norse saw the elder futhark drop from 24 letters down to 16 across Scandinavia, with the 'a' turning into an 'ó', hence the change to futhork. This also divided the evolution of the symbol shapes across regions into the two most common variants; long-branch and short-twig runes.

In England however, as the language developed into Old English, the elder futhark, instead of shrinking, expanded into an eventual 30 runes covered by the English Rune Poem (plus a few extras), also changing the 'a' to an 'ó', as well as the 'k' to a 'c' making it futhorc.

The oldest consistent runic alphabet is the elder futhark which is most favoured by people who use them for divination and spellwork today. So much has already been written about their use as an esoteric system, that I have instead chosen to focus on long-branch runes of the younger futhork. Otherwise known as Viking runes, Scandinavian runes, or Danish runes.

Rune meanings for the younger futhork come from the Norwegian Rune Poem, dated to around the 13th century and the Icelandic Rune Poem, dated to around the 15th century, although these poems are probably much older than when they were first scribed. Other things that add meaning can be found in the rune shapes, sounds, and fragments of how they were used historically.

The table below (next page) shows a side-by-side comparison of the elder futhark with the younger futhork and their basic translation with a pronunciation guide for an Australian accent

72 Living Witchery: Divination

Elder Futhark	Name and Pronunciation	Direct Translation	Younger Futhork	Name and Pronunciation	Direct Translation
ᚠ	**Feoh** Fay-oh	Cattle/wealth	ᚠ	**Fé** Feh	Wealth
ᚢ	**Úruz** Ooo-roo-zz	Aurochs (an extinct wild European bison)	ᚢ	**Úr** Oo (like in 'stood')-rr	Slag/dross or rainshower
ᚦ	**Þurisaz** thoo-ri-sahz	Giant/troll/monster	ᚦ	**Þorse** Thorse to rhyme with horse	Giant/troll/monster
ᚨ	**Ansuz** Ahn-s'oo' in stood-zz	Aesir deity/Estuary	ᚭ	**Óss** awe-s	Estuary
ᚱ	**Raiðo** ray-tho	Ride	ᚱ	**Reið** Raythe to rhyme with lathe	Ride
ᚲ	**Kenaz/Kauna** Ken-ahz/Kawn-ah	Blister/sore or torch	ᚴ	**Kaun** Rounded Cow-n to rhyme with a rounded gown	sore/boil
ᚷ	**Gebo** Geb-owe	Gift			
ᚹ	**Wunjo** w-'oo' in stood-n-yo	Joy			
ᚺ	**Hagalaz** Hah-gahl-ahz	Hail	ᚼ	**Hagall** Haggle	Hail
ᚾ	**Nauðiz** Now-thiz	Need	ᚾ	**Nauðr** Now-ther	Need
ᛁ	**Ísa** eesa	Ice	ᛁ	**Íss** ees	Ice

Elder Futhark	Name and Pronunc-iation	Direct Translation	Younger Futhork	Name and Pronunc-iation	Direct Translation
ᛃ	**Jera** year-aah	Harvest	ᛅ	**Ár** ore	Year
ᛇ	**Eiwaz** Ay-wahz/ eye-wahz	Yew tree			
ᛈ	**Perðro** perthe-row	Pear or apple tree, hearth, well, musical instrument, womb, dice-cup, fate			
ᛉ	**Algiz/ Elhaz** Al-giz/ El-haz	Elk			
ᛋ	**Sówiló** sow-wheel-oh	The Sun	ᛋ	**Sól** sol	The Sun
ᛏ	**Tiwaz** tea-wahz	Name of the god Tiw	ᛏ	**Týr** Half way between tier and tour	Name of the god Týr.
ᛒ	**Berkano** Berk-ahn-oh	Birch tree	ᛒ	**Bjarkan** Byar-kahn	Birch tree
ᛖ	**Ehwaz** eh-wahz	Horse			
ᛗ	**Mannaz** mahn-ahz	Man/human	ᛘ	**Maðr** Mahthe-rah	Man/human
ᛚ	**Laguz/ Laukr** Lah-gooz/ law-kuh	Lake, leek	ᛚ	**Lögr** Law-guh	Natural running water

Elder Futhark	Name and Pronunc-iation	Direct Translation	Younger Futhork	Name and Pronunc-iation	Direct Translation
◇	**Ingwaz** Ing-wahz	Seed, name of the god/king/ancestor Invyfreyr aka Fróði and Freyr	ᛦ	**Ýr** Half way between ear and air Eee-rr	Yew tree
ᛞ	**Dagaz** Dahg-ahz	Day			
ᛟ	**Oþila / Oþala** Othil-ah/ Oath-ah-la	Inherited property			

Making your own runes

Rune sets have become readily available these days in an array of materials and it is perfectly fine to buy a set of ready-made staves. If you are a little crafty then you might like to make your own out of ethically sourced shell, bone, wood, pebbles, or clay. However, if you want to get started straight away, there is nothing wrong with creating a temporary set out of some stiff cardboard.

Like with any divination tool, you will need to bond with them. Traditionally this would have included using a drop of blood during stave construction, but it is not necessary. Sleep with them under your pillow, handle them regularly, talk to them and sing their names, all of this will help you to bond with them and learn their meanings. You also want to make sure they have a 'home' such as a bag or box.

Reading the runes

The two most common methods of runic divination are to lay out a spread as you would do for Tarot or to cast them freeform. I prefer the casting method outlined below. Some like to use elaborately drawn casting boards designed for their own personal way of reading, but a simple cloth shall suffice.

Hold all the runes in your hands and shake them while concentrating on your question. Call their names to wake them up. Inhale deeply, then exhale into the runes, this gift of breath is an energy exchange that creates the personal link to their wisdom. Cast them gently onto your cloth.

The sight in front of you might look like gibberish at first but as you become more familiar with the runes you will see associations and patterns with how they land. The reading is loosely divided into three sections – see the next image.

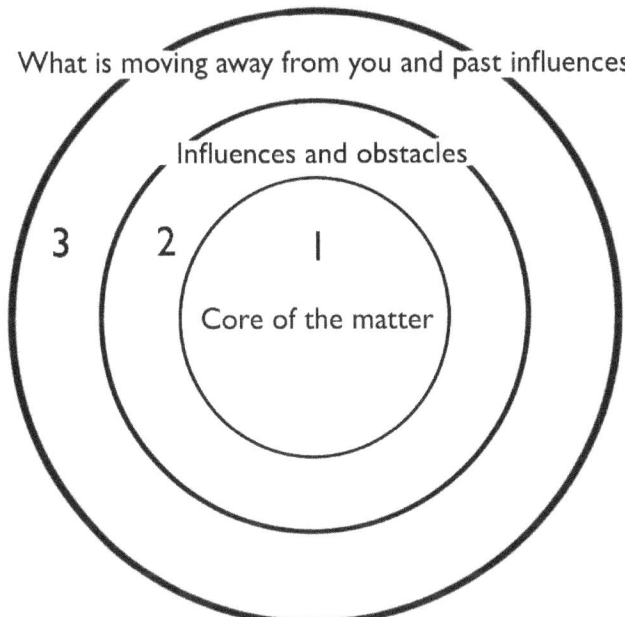

The cast is divided into three sections:
1. The core of the reading
2. Obstacles and influences
3. Past influences that are moving away from you.

Take note of the staves that are face up. Then take note of any staves that are 'hidden', these are the ones that have fallen face up but are hidden underneath other runes.

The central circle is what is important right now. The runes in this section are the absolute core of the reading and will affect how you read the others. If this space is blank, then it is just as important. It may indicate a general inquiry, or it may be that the influences are hidden from the person seeking guidance.

The next circle contains all influences affecting the core. These may be current, moving towards you or moving away. Runes closer to the centre have an imminent effect if you continue on your current course. Rune further away from the core indicate influences which are moving away from the question at hand.

The outer circle represents what has already moved away from you, things that have significantly influenced you in the past, which you have broken away from or you are trying to leave behind.

The 'hidden' rune positions mean the same as the others, but they indicate that all the facts are unknowable at this time, things you are unaware of or choosing to ignore. They also may represent invisible barriers within your subconscious which are preventing you from moving forward. In this method, 'reverse' runes do not apply. Instead, a reverse meaning must be considered through relevance to other runes in deciding which way to read it.

Read the meanings of the individual runes and ask yourself: How do their meanings work together? Do they clash or support each other? Do they seem relevant to the core?

It helps to draw the cast on a piece of paper and overlay the three circles. This also allows you to mark connections between them and take notes. Refer to the following image for an example of a simple rune reading.

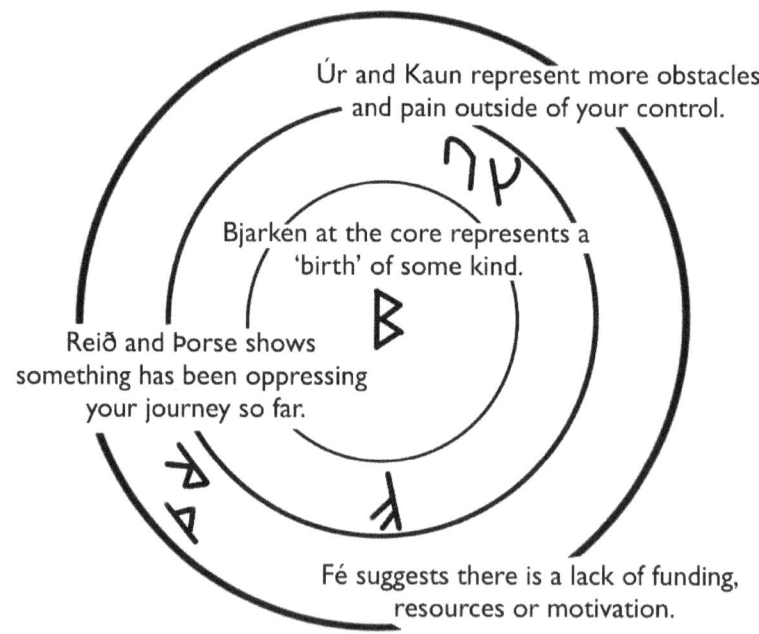

In the centre is Bjarkan, suggesting the 'birth' of something, most likely a business or large project of some kind. Úr and Kaun are together suggesting that there are painful obstacles in your life getting in the way of starting this project. Fé suggests that the main obstacle or limitation is finances. The past influences are Reið and Þorse, suggesting that it has been a very painful journey up to this point.

In entirety, it looks like a warning from the divine spirit to reassess where you are now and to re-evaluate your plans. Look at things from a different perspective and see if there is another path to your goal or another option to access resources. Alternatively, reassess your goal and consider if it was realistic and achievable in the first place.

Rune Meanings

ᚠ Fé

Wealth

Wealth creates a set of unique problems. It can feed greed and selfishness in those who have it and foster feelings of jealousy and bitterness in those who don't. Wealth can generate a complete lack of empathy for fellow humans in times of need. This rune is both a blessing, referring to money coming in or being materially secure, but it is also a warning about greed and mistreating people to attain that wealth.

In a reading, Fé directly relates to wealth. It may be material wealth but it may be something else entirely which can enrich your life such as experiences, love or inspiration. The surrounding runes will give clues about the form of this wealth. Ask yourself if you are using your wealth wisely?

ᚢ Úr

Shower/dross

Úr is slag from the forge and also a shower of rain. This rune is all about separating the excrement from the sugar in life – the slag from the good iron. It highlights the importance of understanding that we are not in control of everything and sometimes the timing is just wrong. We must make a conscious effort to evaluate the situation and see if we can change negative, detrimental influences, or if it is something out of our control that we just have to work with.

Úr is about obstacles and delays. This rune is telling you to honestly assess your obstacles and understand that life is not always perfect. It is what it is. It tells you to stop beating yourself up because you're not what you think you 'should' be or that you haven't achieved what you set out to do. Ask yourself what is in your way? Have you objectively analysed your life and identified where you wish to welcome change?

Þ Þorse
Giant/Troll/Monster

Þorse is the rune of Þursar, which are giants, trolls, or monsters. More accurately, þursar can be understood as primordial beings without consciousness or conscience, as such they represent a deep unconscious shadow influence. The rune poems directly state that it is the 'anguish of women', drawing attention to any issues that have traditionally been unique to women or those who identify as women. It may indicate physical trouble with pregnancy, conception and birth, menstrual health, toxic feminism, sexism or even domestic violence or unhealthy relationships. Spiritually, it may be an indication of the negative influences of the shadow self. This is the rune of oppression in all its forms.

Þorse in a reading is really a warning rune to be on the lookout for hidden dangers. It suggests that there is an interfering, harmful influence over the situation that you have previously not been aware of. This rune usually puts a negative slant on the meaning of the other runes close by. Do you have deep seated issues that repeatedly resurface in your life? Do you self-sabotage? Is there someone else who has toxic behaviour in your life or are you the toxic one? This rune may also indicate struggles with mental illness.

ᚮ Óss
Estuary

Óss is an estuary, where rivers and streams flow into the ocean. The water is brackish. It is not quite the ocean and not quite the river. As such, this is a place of transitioning, a symbolic 'liminal space'. It is where a sea voyage begins and where it returns home, signifying a decision that must be made whether to go out to sea or to stay safely near home. The water is symbolic of inspiration of the spirit and there is balance in the movement, rather than an exact equilibrium. It represents a place of waiting, but waiting in the estuary is not stagnant. There is a lot happening even if it doesn't feel like it. The Icelandic Rune Poem tells us this is also the rune of the 'Prince of Asgard' and 'Lord of Valhalla' which refers to none other than Odin. Odin's functions in relation to Óss are that of ecstatic trance and inspiration. This is what is swirling in the water of the estuary.

In a reading, Óss is a pausing point waiting for the inspiration of the divine to hit. It's time to decide if you will embark on the journey, go home, or simply hang around in limbo for a while longer. It tells you to be open to messages from the divine and to enjoy the movement of the river of inspiration. What is the Universe saying to you?

ᚱ Reið

Ride

This rune is your ride. Representing journeys, movement and means of transportation. It is about the journey itself, not necessarily the destination. The experience of living is not always linear but instead may be spiralling. This rune may appear if you have a repeated pattern of behaviour, finding yourself in the same situations repeatedly – because you, as the traveller, have not paid enough attention to the lessons along the way. The horse you have been riding is tired and on automatic pilot. It knows the journey inside out, but you, the rider, seem oblivious that you have come this way many times before. In this way, the horse can be seen as a part of our subconscious, driving us in ways we are not aware of. It's time to drag that horse out of the shadows and objectively look.

This rune can be read literally or symbolically. It might indicate transport problems or an emotional or spiritual journey. For good or ill, it is at least movement. The surrounding runes will indicate the direction you should be exploring. Basically, it is time to look at your life from the perspective of the rider and the horse.

ᚴ Kaun

Ulcer/Boil

This rune translates to an ulcer, sore, or boil and the poems specifically refer to children. As an ulcer or sore, it indicates pain. It may be that a lot of things have been bubbling under the surface for some time, culminating in a boil that shall surely burst. It may be a physical manifestation, or it may be an outpouring of emotion. Kaun is painful but also cathartic and necessary for growth. When it does finally burst, healing can begin.

Kaun may be referring to literal children in your life who are going through something difficult such as illness, learning difficulties, or bullying. Or it may be drawing attention to your own inner child. Kaun may also be the culmination of many toxic thoughts, behaviours and situations that finally come to a head and explode. The influence is from within rather than external. Do you keep everything bottled up? What does your inner child need right now?

✳ Hagall

Hail

Haggall is being bombarded by hailstones. It is external forces that come hard and fast, and it may be painful. Sometimes this relentless attack is exactly what you need to draw attention to the situation for it to change. Haggall is obvious and immediate rather than a gradual worsening of the situation. It may be likened to the symbolism of The Tower card in Tarot. The poems refer to Hagall as 'the coldest of grain' implying a sense of nourishment. Hail strips plants of their leaves and destroys new seedlings. However, as the ice melts, it rejuvenates the soil, allowing the moisture to deeply penetrate the earth. In this way, it is an emotional earthing rune. It draws attention to external forces we have been ignorant of. We can see Hagall as a 'cruel to be kind' rune, coming hard and fast, stripping away all that we have outgrown.

In a reading, Hagall indicates the final overload of external influences. It tells you it is time to face the reality you're in and decide if you honestly want to stay getting hit with the ice or if it's time to let the ice melt to healing water. Whatever is going on right now can no longer be ignored – time to make some changes.

✝ Nauðr

Need

Nauðr is need. This is the rune of proverbially pushing dung uphill. Sometimes you might feel like you are doing so much work all the time and never getting anywhere for your efforts. Nauðr really draws attention to your physical reality. Are your basic human needs being met? Do you have somewhere to live, a coat to keep you warm in winter, and a shady spot to sit in summer? Do you have a full fridge or the means to fill it? Do you have meaningful relationships with people? Do you feel like you are lacking something necessary for living? Are you deeply craving something?

This rune in a reading is telling you to really examine what it is you feel you need to survive and what you deeply desire to feed your soul. Perhaps you have been punishing yourself lately or depriving yourself of something. It is time to address this feeling that something is missing and work out if it truly is necessary to feel this way. The surrounding runes will help to sort out what area of your life you may have been neglecting.

ᛁ Ís

Ice

Ís is ice. Not the solid ice of a glacier or hail stone, but rather the thin, icy skin that forms on the top of liquid. In the poems, it is the 'bark of rivers' and 'roof of the wave', as such it is a temporary pause of the usual movement and flow of the river.

When this rune turns up in a reading it is time to pause and look through that layer of ice to see what is underneath. It indicates you are in a precarious position and any small movement could cause the thin ice to shatter or crack, breaking the illusion of stability. While you are there on the surface, you can look deeper into the situation and seek clarity. You can see through the ice into the water below. You're in a moment of stillness, allowing you to look momentarily with the objective eye of the observer rather than a participant. Think about your situation using your head and not your heart, take a moment and take a breath, but no more than that. Time is of the essence here, do not dawdle, lest the ice shatter and plunge you into the deep cold waters.

ᛅ Ár

Year

Ár literally means year representing seasons and cycles. This rune is closely related to the god Freyr in his functions of fertility and agriculture. Symbolically, this rune is about planting seeds and the eventual harvest, the promise of rewards for hard work, and a reminder that life is always moving – so many cycles working in a beautiful symbiotic dance of life.

When Ár shows up in a reading, it is drawing attention to timing. When is the right time to plant, harvest, or rest? If you plant seeds, then patience is key to enjoying the harvest, but you must actually plant the seeds, or nothing will ever grow. Recognise divine timing. If you've planted the seeds and you know you have done everything in your power to manifest something, but still aren't seeing results, then honestly assess the work you put in towards your goal. If you feel you have done all you could, then it must be surrendered to the mystery of divine timing. This rune may also indicate a fertility issue – such as pregnancy, birth or trouble conceiving.

ᛋ Sól

The Sun

Sól is the sun and another name for Sunna, the Heathen Goddess of the Sun. This is Her rune. This rune represents typical 'masculine' qualities associated with solar energy such as assertiveness, protection, strength, and courage – which to ancient heathens were just as much 'feminine' qualities. However, the symbolism here is more about the divine illumination that accompanies the Sun, much like the Sun card in Tarot. It is all about joy, warmth, and clarity. An 'ah ha' moment is surely about to happen, and everything will make sense.

The sun is essential for life, but in Australia it is also vital to respect it, especially during long hot summers where fire danger, sunburn, and heatstroke are common. So too, it is important to respect the rune of Sól, do not ignore the clarity and illumination that this rune has gifted to you – it's time for action in this place of clarity and understanding.

ᛏ Týr

The God Týr

Named for the God Týr. Týr has origins that are much older than Oðin and is often suggested to have been androgynous or hermaphroditic. In mythological terms, this dualism is representative of balance, extending to the balance of the scales of justice. It is also a rune of self-sacrifice for the right reasons, doing what must be done for the greater good. This concept comes from Týr's greatest known myth where he sacrificed his hand to bind the chaotic force of the wolf Fenrir. This rune is about claiming order over chaos as much as it is justice. Historically, this rune was used to adorn weapons, jewellery, and the warrior as a charm for protection and victory in battle.

When Týr shows up in a reading, it's drawing attention to the objective truth of the situation. Ask yourself if you are being fair to others, or if you are being disloyal, cruel or manipulative? If you know you have done the wrong thing, it's time to try and make amends or at least forgive yourself and move on. Perhaps someone else is displaying this behaviour and needs to be called out on it. It may also indicate having to give something up as a 'sacrifice' in order to pursue another course of action. While not always comfortable or desired, you need to decide the right thing to do. Be honest!

ᛒ Bjarkan
Birch Tree

Bjarkan is the birch tree. From the same etymological root, meaning to 'shine', most likely in reference to the silvery-white bark, it is also the name of the ancient Germanic goddess Berchta. Berchta was known by other names across regions. By the Viking era, She most closely relates to winter functions of Frija the Beloved. Bjarkan then, is a rune associated with divine goddess energy, linked with birth as well as the cycle that follows, of life, death, and rebirth. As such, it is also a rune of cycles and transformation with a distinct early springtime energy.

There is another aspect to this rune which is often absent from interpretations. That is the direct mention of Loki in the Norwegian Rune Poem. What has Loki got to do with birth and the feminine? When we consider that he is an adept shapeshifter and mother of the eight-legged horse, Sleipnir, then it becomes clear there is an association with birth and transformation. In this way, Bjarkan also may embody a transgender or gender-fluid kind of energy.

In a reading, Bjarken represents the 'mother' in a softer, emotionally nourishing parental role, or a lack thereof, depending on the rest of the reading. Be on the lookout for messages coming through from Goddess. Bjarkan also indicates the beginning or 'birth' of something and the nurturing of that 'baby'. It could be literal or symbolic.

ᛘ Maðr
Man/Human

Maðr means man in the archaic sense, referring to humanity as a whole. The essence of this rune is what it means to be human. It draws attention to elements such as empathy and happiness, as well as sadness and anger, family relationships, friendships, and basic Heathen hospitality. We all have the same basic human needs: water, food, shelter, and companionship. Humans are social creatures by nature, some more so than others, but even the most introverted hermits still need company, conversation and help from time to time. Social interaction is necessary for survival and mental health.

This rune draws attention to our relationships and to our place in society. It is the rune of the collective consciousness of humanity. It also reminds us of our fragility and mortality, our fleeting nature as physical beings of flesh. It tells us we should always strive towards self-improvement, to be better, offer respect to people and treat others as you wish to be treated.

In a reading, this rune may indicate an actual man in your life or one who presents in a traditional masculine way or what you would consider masculine traits. This rune symbolises your personal experience of the human condition and relationship to the divine. It may also be an indication to check on your physical health.

↑ Lögr

Water

Lögr is flowing natural water, like a waterfall, stream, or geyser. This rune takes on all the symbolism associated with flowing water – the emotions, the subconscious, movement, healing, and cleansing. Lögr is running freely, unrestrained, gushing over stone. It shapes and wears away at river stones until they are no longer huge boulders as obstacles in its path, but lovely smooth pebbles that can easily be traversed. This is the power of Lögr – to consistently persevere in the face of challenges and obstacles in life and gradually wear them down into manageable tasks. It is the rune of flow putting an end to stagnation. If you've been stuck in a situation or a mindset, then Lögr brings hope of release through the gushing of the waterfall.

Lögr tells us that whatever has been keeping us stagnant will soon flow again, it is the healing power of freely expressed emotions and the release of subconscious blockages. It is letting go of what we no longer need and allowing the water to flow over us in preparation for the new. Relax a little and surrender.

ᛦ Ýr

Yew

Ýr is the yew tree. The rune poems tell us yew was used for firewood, making bows and arrows, and is the 'giant of the arrow'. I believe the 'giant' is in reference to Skaði (scar-thee) the Jotun goddess and to a lesser extent Ullr (ool-uh to rhyme with wool-uh) the Aesir God of the same function – both considered winter deities associated with bow-hunting. Yew was favoured for making long-bows and arrows because of its flexibility and strength. This suggests being able to bend without breaking, covering the areas of diplomacy and compromise, yet, as the arrow to the bow, it also represents focus.

An extended meaning of the yew tree is the obvious representation as Yggdrasil, the world tree of Heathen cosmology. The shape of this rune also depicts strong roots as the grounding foundation to keep us tethered to reality as we travel to other realms. Notice the link to shamanic practises.

In a reading, Ýr questions your focus and your attitude. It's wonderful to have a goal but you mustn't be too rigid in your approach. There is strength in compromise and flexibility. This rune also draws attention to how grounded you are or if you allow fantasy to rule you. Are you being realistic? Are you (or is someone else) unwilling to compromise?

About Miranda Kopittke
Miranda Kopittke has been a practising witch for almost three decades with specialist knowledge in magical and medicinal use of herbs and rune magic. She is the author of The Nocturne Nook, *a blog covering a range of witchcraft topics with a heavy focus on the arts of seiðr (Germanic magic) as practised in Australia. Miranda has a Bachelor of Arts in Justice Studies and various diplomas in esoteric arts including Advanced Witchcraft and Wicca, Master Herbalist, and Shamanism.*

FACETS: Common or Folk

This section includes divination techniques which are easily accessible and approachable. The methods use everyday or familiar items to inspire psychic readings and gain insights.

Tassology – Tea Leaf Reading

By Jacq Hackett

Let us quieten our minds and leave the busy-ness and noise of the modern world and step into the not-so-distant past.

Imagine the front parlour of a townhouse in post-war England. Normally reserved for special visitors, the room is shut off from the rest of the run-down, stone building. The elegant curtains are pulled closed against the daylight and soft lamplight illuminates the ladies in the room. Esme, 19, glowing with the first blush of pregnancy, still slender and graceful with light brown wavy hair is dressed informally with her starched pinny covering her plain, house dress. She is a beauty. Jenny, her older sister, sits opposite in an occasional chair pouring tea into three delicate cups. She is tiny! Only four foot tall in her stockinged feet, wearing a patched pinafore, with wiry brown hair. Her wizened impish face gives her a quirky appearance. Strange. Mysterious. The sisters' drab manner of dress looks completely out of place in the stylish front room, but Jenny commands the attention of the three well-to-do female guests, sitting nervously across from them.

The room would be silent if not for the clock ticking on the mantle above the fireplace with a young Perry Como crooning on the radio. The nervous excitement of the guests is obvious. They are dressed in their Sunday best, wearing strands of pearls around their necks and pillbox hats upon salon-styled hair. Whilst they look more suited to the polished décor of the parlour room, they are awkwardly seated, full of anticipation.

At a nod from Jenny, Esme rises slowly and elegantly moves to the radio and turns it off.

For the last three generations, the women in my family have thrilled and entertained guests with divination and communing with the departed. According to my mother, Esme was renowned for holding the scariest seances. There is even a rumour that a guest dropped dead during one such session. Little Aunt Jenny (as my great aunt was known to the family) was often stopped in the street by random women to book an afternoon reading. Her private soirees must have been popular.

It makes sense. Tea leaf reading lends itself perfectly to the atmosphere of an intimate gathering rather than noisy public festivals or markets. A fortune-telling tea party at my Little Aunt Jenny's house in the 1940s sounds like it would have been quite an exciting afternoon after the horrors of the war. If the rumours are true, their light-hearted view of magic was quite scandalous. As far as I can tell, both sisters *were* scandalous.

This chapter aims to bridge a 50-year gap where the art of tassology disappeared from mainstream divination. Perhaps it was the introduction of tea bags, perhaps it was the revival of Tarot cards, perhaps it is the immediacy, ease and materialistic nature of modern spiritual expos and market stalls, but modern divination methods rarely include tea leaf reading. The process requires the ingredients be first freshly brewed, then consumed, and lastly, interpreted. Reading tea leaves is not fast enough for today's busy world of instant divination. For those of us who prefer the intimate setting, the time to relax and connect with our intuition, reading tea leaves may offer the modern practitioner a more welcome environment.

The Mirriam-Webster dictionary defines 'tass' from French, Arabic and Scottish languages, as a small, ornamental cup or drinking bowl. Tassology is the art of interpreting images made from tea leaves, coffee grounds or wine sediment remaining in a cup.

Whilst we don't necessarily need a comprehensive checklist of shape meanings, it is fascinating to read the multitude of leaf patterns and associations. Modern online texts reference hundreds of symbols with roots in agricultural Europe, through to 21st century technology. I only learnt a handful of symbols, shapes and interpretations from my Nana and Little Aunt Jenny before they passed.

However, imagery meditation and channelling messages is something I have consciously practiced since I was young. The endless unfocussed gazing at clouds, patterns in 70s linoleum flooring, spaces between leaves on trees all offered shapes and from these shapes I intuited meanings. Even beginner witches who have basic meditation skills can apply their talents to divination via scrying, reading tea leaves and other forms of pattern recognition fortune telling.

So how does one read leaves?

The best kind of tea to use is large, loose-leaf tea. Tea bags, when opened, contain too much dust and the powdery residue won't clump into images and proves too difficult to read. The idea is to have loose leaves left in the cup, so do not use a strainer when pouring the tea. The best cup to use has a wider top opening with a narrower base and a clear, white interior. Mugs are very difficult to read, as the insides are perpendicular, and the symbols cannot be seen properly. I have noticed trendy tassology cups with astrological signs printed on the inside being advertised. I love the look of these but am not well versed in astrology. For me, the printed symbols only obscure the patterns made by the leaves and do not add value to my reading. Of course, if astrology *is* your cup of tea, this could add another layer of meaning for your client.

Once your querent is seated comfortably with their tea, ask them to focus on their question as they drink. It is perfectly normal to have a conversation. Their question will remain in their subconscious and keep resurfacing as they drink. The aim is to relax. Both of you. Notice the way your client sits, holds their cup, and drinks. If the client is relaxed to the point where you could mistake the conversation as a catch up between old friends, their energy will flow freely from thoughts to emotions and physiological changes in their body. If the client is tense, top up their cup, join them in a drink and chat.

For a good reading, we need less than half a teaspoonful of tea remaining in the bottom of the cup. If the client can't finish the last mouthful, invite them to carefully and slowly, invert the cup. You may wish to have a saucer, bowl, or other vessel to catch the liquid. The ancient Greeks used to use violent splashes of wine to divine messages of love. We do not. As the reader, retrieve the upended cup carefully and turn it gently, anticlockwise with your left hand, three times. If you are naturally left-handed, please use your right hand, clockwise. This action helps with draining the last of the liquid, it represents casting a circle, and it focuses the practitioner's mind on the cup. Turn the cup the right way up and peer inside.

To the untrained eye, the leaves formed in the bottom and sides of the cup will appear to be a seemingly meaningless confusion of circles, dots, lines, and clumps. Hold the cup closely and turn it about looking for anything you recognise. This part is akin to scrying. Once you identify a shape, look for more. Keep rotating the cup to view the leaves from different angles. Do not worry if you cannot make out any shapes. Invite the client to look as well. An image may jump out from the surrounding leaves when one is asked to 'think' about their question. Brains are wired to distinguish patterns, so it is highly unlikely you won't see something you recognise.

I recently read for a friend who didn't ask a specific question. Instead, he was open to a bit of fun. If this is the case with your client, their mind won't be switched on. They will rely on you to identify an event that is likely to influence their life. I seem to always find something inconsequential to share with them, but sometimes I see a clear symbol with an important message. I try not to jump to the worst possible scenario, even if it seems glaringly obvious.

My friend had leaves in the shape of a boot missing the toe area and an aeroplane. I asked if he was planning a trip away. He was. I mentioned he may need a flexible ticket or insurance due to possible luggage issues. He ended up postponing his trip after falling and injuring his leg. Revelations like this stress me. I remember my mother saying the same of Little Aunt Jenny when she blurted out, "Oh Ez! There's a broken ring!" Two weeks later my Grandpop died whilst still in the prime of his life.

Please do not tell your client they will die. In Tarot, I have turned over the Death card with the Tower, the Devil and 10 of Swords in a single reading. It was a challenging time for me but I'm still alive. The imagery is always open to interpretation, especially timewise.

Where the shapes form in the cup affects their timing. The handle is considered the client's homebase or present moment. From this fixed point, with the handle facing you, imagery to the left of the handle represents journeys away from home, messages the client needs to compose or activities they need to start. If closer to the rim of the cup, the event is urgent or will occur quickly. Leaves at the bottom of the cup represent the far future. If shapes form on the walls of the cup, the event is sometime in between. The nearer the symbols are to the handle on the right-hand side, the closer these events are to being completed. These represent return journeys or visits from others, messages received, and goals fulfilled.

Look for actual pictures, numbers, and letters. The larger and clearer they are, the more certain you can be of the interpretation. In my Grandpop's case, the broken ring was clear, prominent and near the rim. All else at the bottom of the cup was obscured and of little importance no matter how lucky the symbols may have been.

The most common questions querents ask deal with being lucky in something. Typical questions are "Will I get a new job?", "Will I get married to X?", or "Will I be successful in Y?" Here, the placement of the symbols will help regarding the timeframe. There are usually no clear yes/no answers in reading tea leaves. More often the practitioner will see dots on the bottom of the cup (representing reward in the distant future) and the answer will be, "If you get a new job, you won't see a financial reward for quite some time", or, "If you marry X, you will eventually come into an inheritance", or, "No, not in the short term. But stick with it and you will."

With leaves at the bottom of the cup, the actual time frame could be five or fifty years. Stating the far future will serve the client better than giving a date. Numbers, like letters, are guiding images. They assist the client in recognising opportunities when they see them. For example, rather than confirming they will marry X in two years when a clear numeral is present, ask the querent if they know a person associated with the number two. This could be someone born in the second month (February), or in a year that ends with two (1992, 2002, etc). Perhaps the love match lives at number two, or their phone number ends in two.

In my own case, versions of 196 were foretold as my important numbers ten years ago. I was mistaken in believing these numbers identified my now ex-husband as 'The One'. He was born 09.01.1966. My current life partner, Dan, was born the exact same day (and yes, that was a surprise when I discovered the date). Unlike my previous marriage, those numbers, one, nine and six were prominent from the outset: Dan and I met on 19th October 2019, live at number 16, and his phone number ends in 69.

Let the querent sit with the numbers as a guide only. They will make more sense to them in time.

The interpretation of tea leaf imagery is much like Tarot and dream symbols. It comes down to surrounding symbols. When the reader is tuned into their intuition and is experienced in connecting multiple shapes with meanings, a full story is revealed. Generations of readers have associated the appearance of certain shapes with the occurrence of certain events. This intuitive knowledge has been handed down and passed on to others, as I am doing here. The following short list of shapes contains the symbology I use when reading tea leaves.

Symbol	Left of handle	Right of handle
Acorn	From little things, big things grow. A seed of an idea needs to be nurtured and it will produce great results. Start small but start.	Think again about the project. Results may be smaller than expected. Pause. Review.
Anchor	A slow start to a project. Something will hold you back. A good, solid reason for staying where you are.	A project will come to halt. Stop. Take a break. Review the situation.
Arrow	Send a message even if you are uncomfortable with the information. Pay attention to your words and actions.	You will receive some uncomfortable news. Be alert.
Axe	You are about to go through a challenging time. Life will change.	You will overcome a challenging time. The fight will end.
Birds	You are going on a journey. You have good news to share.	You will have a successful journey. You receive good news.

Symbol	Left of handle	Right of handle
Bridge	Make things right. If the bridge is broken, you end a relationship	A friend will return. If the bridge is broken, the relationship ends.
Butterfly	Success is fleeting. Enjoy it while it lasts.	Success is fleeting. Enjoy it while it lasts.
Cart, wheelbarrow	Lean times ahead. Prepare.	Wealth and fortune approaches.
Chain	Commit to the decision. If the chain is broken, it's not a wise choice.	You are locked into your choice. If the chain is broken, you are released from obligation.
Circles	Spend money or time with someone you love. A broken circle means you will lose money or your loved one.	You will receive a gift from someone you love. A broken circle means you will receive an unpleasant surprise.
Clover	Always lucky, especially if it has four leaves.	Always lucky, especially if it has four leaves.
Coffin	Sickness.	A close friend is gravely ill.
Cross	Trouble ahead. Try to get out of whatever you have planned. Delays.	Disruption. Chaos. The end of a project.
Flowers	Success. A happy marriage. A new baby. Joy and good times ahead.	A friend will apologise or wish you well.
Hand	Give. Be generous and kind.	Receive gratitude or help.
Heavenly bodies (sun, moon, stars)	Yes. You are the maker of dreams come true. Success.	Yes. You will receive the answer to all your dreams. Success.
Ring	You will fall in love. A broken ring means the relationship will not last. If close to the rim, a quick flirt.	A long and loving marriage or relationship. A broken ring means the relationship will end. If close to the rim, a sudden end.
Shoes	You will leave on a journey.	You will return safely.
Sword	Victory in an argument or debate. A broken sword means you don't have the right information. Confusion.	You will be defeated in an argument. A broken sword means someone has the wrong information. Confusion.

While this list is a brief selection of the vast array of symbols you will encounter in your cup, it is a tantalising appetizer for developing your own dictionary of symbols. As mentioned earlier, there are hundreds of shapes and symbols recorded in online resources stretching from archaic objects to the ultra-modern. If you associate travel with an aeroplane and see leaves forming the image in a cup, knowing the position from the handle and the rim will give further meaning. If you associate the @ symbol with emails and communication and see it in someone's teacup, consider the position and determine if the client needs to send a message or if they are to receive one. It is ultimately up to the reader to use their intuition to divine a client's fortune.

Researching what information is available to budding fortune tellers on the internet, I consulted Google, The All-Wise. My belief was the modern witch, short on time and with ready access to the wide world web could use pattern recognition software bundled nicely in an app to read and translate images.

I did find a simple cup reading app to upload pictures of used coffee cups. If you are prepared to wait ten minutes and watch the in-app advertisements, the AI reader prepares a very short, generic fortune. There are options to use the app's coffee cups (if you do not have one of your own to read) or select the horoscope section for an alternative reading. Another app I found did not provide any assistance in translating tea leaf images into meanings. It merely connected the user to the app creator's horoscope page after some arbitrary information on tassology. To busy witches and budding tea leaf readers, there is no technological shortcut, yet.

With practice, the art of divination will become easier. So sit back and enjoy your next cup of tea.

About Jacq Hackett

Jacq Hackett is an international speaker, mindset coach and practising witch, as featured in Living Witchery Beginner Witch Guide *(published 2021). Transforming businesses in the leadership development space, Jacq uses scientific, metaphysical and quantum principles in NLP, manifestation, and the Law of Attraction. Her workshops break through subconscious self-sabotage and uncover hidden potential. Using the* Quantum Reset Method *(and a little magick), Jacq helps propel success from slow to sensational.*

It's All in Your Hands

By Scarlet Paige

For my mother who fostered my love of divination

As a young girl, I would often attend local markets with my mother and it is here that I began a lifelong love affair with divination. As we wandered about the various stalls, inevitably we'd find a reader who would offer to tell us our future. When my mother allowed me to have my cards or palm read, I would listen with interest about what wonderous things awaited me.

As I got older, I became more and more interested in divination. When I turned 16, I asked a local reader to teach me palmistry. This was a milestone moment. More than three decades on, I continue to apply those teachings and learn more all the time. The best advice I have for anyone starting out is to go with your instincts.

To become an adept palm reader can take years as there are many ways to read and each has its own contradictions. Just like any divination method, you will find variations on how to read palms. How I read and interpret the hands and the lines will be similar but also different to other palmists. This one chapter is not enough to allow for an in-depth dive into the complexities of the palm and the many lines, marks, positions and nuances; however, I will share many basic skills so you can begin your own journey into palmistry if you choose.

Your hands tell a story, a story of your past, present and future. Since the stone age, hands have been used to express ourselves. They have been drawn on cave walls and used in dance. Many cultures and societies have some form of palmistry as a divination technique. You may first think of palmistry associated with the widely travelled Romani people. However, when you research palmistry, the history goes far back to ancient India, Greece, Rome, Italy, and Russia where palmistry was practised in various ways.

Mystics and seers who charged for their predictions told tales of fairies and demons who feared precious metals such as silver, gold, or iron. Therefore, those who wished to have a reading would make the sign of the cross over a palm reader's hand with a coin, and be protected. Of course, it seemed reasonable that the coin was kept as a token of thanks as fortunes were told.

Which hand should I read?

This question has been asked for as long as people have been reading palms. Some say the right hand shows the present and future, whereas the left hand shows the past and events that have made the querent who they are today.

Others only read the right, totally ignoring the left. I ask clients which is their dominant hand and read that. If the querent is right-handed, read the right; if left-handed, read the left. If during the reading I feel there is something missing, out of place or unseen, then I may ask to see the other hand to assist in clarification.

It's up to you whether you sit opposite or beside the querent.

The following information may not be true in all circumstances or for everyone. There are always outliers and people who don't fit into 'average'.

How the hands are presented

The way a querent presents their hand is as important as how the fingers are held. If a querent presents their hands to you palms up, with fingers wide, they are showing that they are open, honest, and willing to try new things. They are likely to enjoy social activities and are happy-go-lucky.

If a querent presents hands to you palms down, fingers closed (either in a fist or fingers held closely together) they are more likely to be closed off, introverted, perhaps shy or timid. They may not enjoy being on display and may prefer to watch rather than participate in activities. They could be more cautious and careful in their interactions with others.

There are various interpretations of hand sizes and their relationship with the querent's outlook on life. I personally do not use the size of hands but encourage you to do further research if you find the concept interesting.

Firmness and feel of hands

The density/firmness and feel of a querent's hands can help you determine if they are able to handle the challenges life will throw at them.

Firm coarse hands

The owners of firm coarse hands respond well to challenges and stress. They are usually capable and do well in difficult and crisis situations. They make excellent leaders and tend to have an authority about them. If the skin is also coarse and heavy, the person is likely to have lots of energy and go on when others have given up. This energy can build up and become negative if not released. They are usually independent thinkers who enjoy being in charge. They surround themselves with people and even when winding down seem to be full of energy.

Soft gentle hands

People with soft hands may find dealing with stress more challenging and can prefer to have others take the lead. They are usually excellent support people due to being empathetic. They often sympathise with others. They are natural carers and healers who enjoy helping others. Although people with soft gentle hands can appear to be more emotional and reactive at times, they notice small details and ensure plans are executed correctly. They usually turn inward to relax and enjoy reading or watching a play or movie. People with soft gentle hands do need to be alone at times to wind down.

Shape of the palm

The shape of the palm can be difficult to determine. Look at the hand with the palm facing upward, ignoring the fingers. There are several different ways to categorise the hand. Some readers use up to seven different shapes, but I find this confusing and prefer a simpler method of three categories – square, oblong/rectangle, or round.

Square

A square hand is about the same size vertically as it is horizontally. These hands are easy to spot by the squarish corners at the base of the palm and tops of the hand. People with square hands are usually practical, logical, and determined. They prefer quick answers to questions and are not really interested in lots of details unless these are vital to the conversation. They are hardworking and often work in physical or high-energy roles. At their worst, the owners of square palms are stubborn, but at their best they can drive change and get things back on track when they have stalled.

Oblong/rectangular

An oblong hand (also known as a rectangular hand) is longer than it is wide.

People with this shape hand are usually receptive, intuitive, and sensitive. They are more likely to be spiritually focused with the heart and soul of a dreamer. They are often thoughtful and considerate, thinking of others before themselves. However, people with oblong hands can find it difficult to make challenging decisions alone and benefit from having a sounding board. They have amazing imaginations and come up with great ideas. The owners of an oblong hand are the inventors and creators of the world. It is important that their work/career has variety and purpose to ensure they stay engaged.

Round
A round hand may seem squarish at first, as the top near the fingers can be square but at the base of the hand the bottom corners are more rounded. Round handed individuals are usually happy, easy-going and enjoy life. They are popular with others and are warm and friendly. They are the glue in any group, a lynchpin who others enjoy being around. They are usually flexible in all things and can lead or follow. They will take charge when needed, but their biggest downside is that they can be people pleasers.

Finger length
For simplicity, fingers can be categorised as short, medium, or long. Consider the length of the fingers in relation to the length of the palm. If the fingers are shorter than the palm, they are short. Longer than the palm, they are long and obviously, if in the middle, they are medium.

Short fingers
Those with short fingers tend to be more centred on self. They often like to find the answers quickly and can be impatient and impulsive. They tend to prefer the big picture of any task or activity rather than the details. People with short fingers can often have more than one thing happening at once and they are good at multitasking. Short fingered people may give anything a go but may be challenged by intricacies.

Medium fingers Those with medium fingers are a mix of the traits of short and long fingered. They can be patient, but they can also be impulsive. They may like details on some things but big picture on others. For them to be engaged, they must enjoy the topic. People with medium-length fingers are more changeable, and their moods change easily. They may find themselves moving between the characteristic listed with little warning.

Long fingers

Those with long fingers tend to be considerate, patient, and sensitive. They like details and information in all they do and are happy to take time to absorb it all. People with long fingers are creative and artistic. Their minds are constantly busy, and this is the way they like it. Their work needs to be interesting and ever changing or they get bored. They love to sort out messes and make great problem solvers.

Fingertip shape
Square

Someone with square tips on their fingers is practical and hardworking. They have lots of energy and enjoy working in physical pursuits. They like to follow rules and enjoy the outdoors. People with square fingertips enjoy doing things that challenge them physically. They can be conservative but are reliable, and don't usually enjoy change unless it is necessary.

Round

The round fingertip querent is flexible and adaptable. They are happy to be either inside or outdoors if they are with others. They don't need routine or structure but can work within it when necessary. They tend to bring out the best in others and make good leaders, as they are caring and empathetic.

Pointed

The querent with pointed fingertips can be emotional, intuitive, and sensitive. They are more easily influenced by the emotions of others and may feel overwhelmed when in large groups. They prefer the company of a limited number of people at one time. People with pointed fingertips usually enjoy routines but can be daydreamers.

Fingernails
Large nails

People with large nails are usually strong and enjoy the outdoors and physical activities. They like to create and make things and are often found in tradie roles or have a hobby as an outlet for excess energy.

Small nails

Someone with small nails is likely to enjoy the finer things in life. They like luxuries and enjoy spending time with others. They do well in jobs which require mixing with people. However, people with small nails can find their energy lacking at times and need time to recuperate and re-energise.

The Thumb
The thumb relates to one's will, ego and life force, and is of great importance in any palmistry reading.

Thumb length
The size of a thumb is a good indicator of personal success. The bigger or longer the thumb, the bigger the ego and will of the querent. A large thumb can be a determiner of success in business. A short thumb may mean the querent is happy to go with the flow and not push for their own way. They can still be successful but are usually much less assertive.

Thumb width
The width of the thumb is also a good indicator of will or force of nature. The wider the thumb, the more determined the person may be. A thin thumb can relate to a querent who may be flightier and more confused at times, but it can also show great creativity and artistic ability.

Flexibility and angle of the thumb
The size of the angle between the querent's index finger and thumb is indicative of their friendliness, generosity and flexibility. If the angle is 90 degrees or more, they will be easy going and generous. The smaller the angle, the less flexible and generous and the more stubborn and immoveable they will likely be.

Types of hand
Square short – square palms and short fingers
People with this type of hand are logical, practical, and usually just want to get the job done. They are hardworking and don't mind manual jobs that others may find too challenging.

These people are a friend to the end, reliable and trustworthy. When they say they will do something, it gets done and it's difficult to stop a person with square short hands once in motion. At times, they can be impatient, but if given simple reasons for something they can be persuaded to change their mind.

Square long – square palms and long fingers
Those with square long hands enjoy logic and like to have a reason for things they do. They do not rely on gut instinct. The owners of square long hands enjoy talking to others and can be very convincing when necessary. They may enjoy working in a job where they can discuss things deeply. They are rational and can be very passionate about family and friends. Square long hand people do like to have a plan and are not one to do things spontaneously.

Oblong short – oblong/rectangular palms and short fingers
People with these kind of hands go at a thousand miles an hour. They have lots of ideas and more than one iron in the fire. Ideas flow out of them continually and they may find it hard to know where to start or finish, therefore staying on task can be difficult. Oblong short hand people can get caught up in emotions and carried away, becoming impatient and impulsive. They are, however, never dull and when at their best are inspiring and motivating, seeing the best in everything.

Oblong long – oblong/rectangular palms and long fingers
The owners of oblong long hands feel things very strongly, and how others are feeling is important to them. They dwell on any mistake and can be extremely sensitive. Sometimes, they overthink things and lose focus on the objective. Oblong long hands people enjoy a challenge, and can often take on the world's problems, but this makes them a wonderful listener and friend. They have a bountiful imagination that at times has no end and need to be in a job where they feel they are making some difference.

Round short – round palms and short fingers
These people are interested in being happy and are often found in roles that are more about lifestyle than money. They like meeting new people and have a huge circle of friends – some close, others as acquaintances. Round short hand people can lead others but do not necessarily like to be in charge. They enjoy spending time with people close to them. When focused on something and then distracted, they can become annoyed or irritated and lash out at others and are then be immediately sorry. Sometimes, they feel guilty when things are not their fault.

Round long – round palms and long fingers
Individuals with round long hands enjoy people but prefer a few close friends. Other people are often drawn to round long hand people, as they enjoy how

they feel in their company. Round long hand people may have various groups of friends and like to keep them separated from each other. People will often ask round long hand people for their opinions and ideas as they can think outside the box when needed and solve difficult problems with new insights and creative ideas. They are patient and like to have all the information before making decisions.

Major lines on the hand

Depending upon where you learn palmistry, you will hear debate regarding the number of major lines to consider during a palmistry reading. Some say there are four major lines, while others review as many as six. My preferred method uses only three major lines on the palm, as they are easy to find and identify. These major lines are the life line, heart line, and head line.

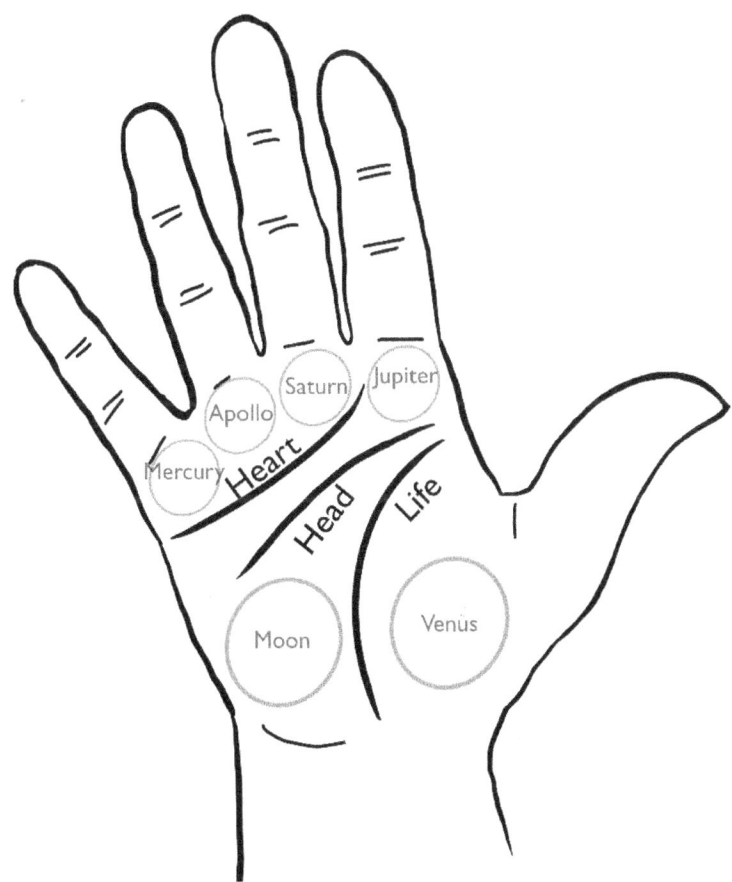

The Life Line
Location of life line
The life line usually starts between the index finger and thumb, and travels in an arc around the mount of Venus toward the base of the hand. If the arc is narrow, it may indicate a lack of energy and drive. The more curved the arc, the more energetic the life. Wide curves are more likely to be found on extroverts and narrow curves on introverts. The thicker or deeper the line, the more grounded to the physical realm the querent will be. A fine line shows the querent may be flighty or nervous and may not be as grounded. The line may stop or fade out but it can also continue to meet up with the lines of the wrist.

Length of life line
Some believe that the length of the lifeline is an indicator of how long a querent will live, but this is only one interpretation and not one I believe. There are many reasons why the line may be short or broken or faint. It can be said that the life line is a determiner of the zest you have for life and how much you get out of life. A reader should not tell a querent that they will have a short life or that they will only live to a certain age. I ignore the length of the line and try to determine what will occur during the life of the querent.

Lines on the mount of Venus
The life line encompasses the mount of Venus and many people have a number of lines running across the mount of Venus. These usually run from the base of the thumb toward the life line. These lines may be worry lines and indicate how much we worry in our lives. If these lines cross over the life line it can be an indicator of a health issue brought on by worry or stress.

Breaks in the life line
If the lifeline is broken or intercepted by other lines, it can be heeded as a warning sign that the health of the querent may need attention. Take this as a warning to make some changes in lifestyle. Ensure the querent knows these concerns are not always serious or life threatening. Breaks in the life line are not necessarily a bad thing and when noted may be a good opportunity to improve health. Small breaks are an indicator of changes that will alter the querent's life in some way.

Sister line/s
Some people have what is called a sister line. This line (or lines) is similar to

the life line but are often inside the main life line. They are usually shorter than the main life line and indicate the querent will be lucky and almost have a second life. Some readers believe it can show a life the querent missed out on or wished they had had but did not due to choices or circumstances.

The heart line
The heart line is associated with your emotions, love, happiness, and contentment. The heart line is a good indicator of how you relate to others in your life. The heart line begins at the outside of the hand under the little finger and crosses the hand, usually ending somewhere under the index or middle finger. The heart line can differ in length and end in different ways.

Long heart line
Sometimes, the heart line can be longer and end further along under the index finger, but this is not common. Where this happens, this querent may love others deeply and without hesitation. They throw everything they have and are into their relationships, and expect the same back. They can, at times, be too demanding and may become suffocating, destroying relationships. These people can, however, also be a partner who will nurture and care for another without question, no matter what.

Medium heart line
A medium heart line ending in between the index and middle finger shows a querent who has reasonable expectations of love and will be caring and emotional but will also be sensible and take time to get to know others. They are balanced and understand that love does not need to be all-consuming but is a wonderful part of life.

Short heart line
A very short line ending before the middle finger may be an indication of someone who struggles to share themselves and their emotions. They may find relationships difficult and struggle to communicate on an intimate level or commit to someone, even when they want to.

Curved or straight heart lines
Heart lines can be either curved or straight. Curved lines show an openness as well as a willingness to show affection and caring for others. These people are willing to communicate and share in hope of working out any issues. Straight lines show the opposite. These people may be more careful in

showing how they feel, are more closed off and less demonstrative in their affections. They may love deeply but struggle to show those emotions to others for fear of rejection. People with a straight heart line may also find it difficult to communicate their feelings.

If an individual has a combination of short and curved, or short and straight, or long and curved, or long and straight, there will be a mix of the above characteristics.

The head line

The head line is to do with our minds, self-confidence and determination as well as how we think. The head line begins near the life line, between the thumb and index finger, usually above the life line. It crosses the hand in a downward arc ending under the line of the ring finger. In some cases, the head line can cross the entire hand and end at the side.

Curved or straight head lines

Head lines are usually curved and show the level of creativity and imagination people have. Those with a strong curve are usually more creative and enjoy some sort of artistic hobby. If the line is quite curved, the querent may struggle to cope with the daily grind of the real world and may like to escape into books or gaming. This is not necessarily a bad thing, as it may be the way they release the stress of their daily lives.

Long head line

A long head line will run across the palm and may end under the pinky finger. A long line can be an indicator of a quick mind and the ability to multitask well. People with a long head line may be able to complete many different tasks and like to keep busy. They have many interests, but none hold their attention long term – a jack of all trades but master of none.

Medium head line

A medium head line may mean a person who is able to consider all aspects of tasks and chose the best option for the greatest outcome. They seem to always make the right decision and things fall into place for them. This is not by chance, but due to taking time to consider possibilities before making decisions. They are sensible, thoughtful, good with detail, and able to complete a task well.

Short head line
A shorter head line means someone who likes to focus on one thing at a time and doing it well. They are usually very good at completing a specific task from beginning to end, before beginning another. They struggle to multitask.

Starting point of the head line
Where the head line starts will be a good indicator of how confident a person is and how sure they are of their abilities. It shows how much drive they have to take make things happen. The head line can start in a few ways:
1. *Inside the mount of Venus.* When the head line starts inside the mount of Venus and beneath the life line, this shows the person is introverted and may have difficulty expressing their ideas. They have the desire to speak up but find it hard. These people can be emotional and quiet at times, which can be to their detriment.
2. *At the same place as the life line.* If the head line starts in the same place as the life line, family and relationships are of great importance, and this person's heart can rule their head. At times, they may make decisions not based on logic but on emotions.
3. *Above the life line.* It is common for most head lines to start above the life line. When this occurs, the gap between the life and head line is important. When someone's head line starts above their life line, the gap between the two will indicate how confident and determined they are. The bigger the gap, the more confidence and determination they will have.

The writer's fork
Most head lines will end in one line but not all. There are cases where the head line ends by spitting into a fork. This ending is found in those who have a great imagination and can utilise it, such as writers, storytellers, and artists who rely on their imagination to create stories, paintings, or songs. This fork is a symbol of an active and vivid imagination that can be harnessed and used.

The palmar crease or Simian line
This feature appears when the heart and head lines are merged into one single thick line across the palm. The palmar crease (also known as Simian line) is rare, found in less than 5% of people. This line can be considered in two ways.

When viewed through a positive lens, people with a palmar crease are focused, intelligent, confident, determined, and ambitious. When viewed with a negative lens, they may be aggressive, stubborn, inconsiderate, arrogant, and selfish. Alternatively, this line can indicate the head and heart are fused into one and a constant struggle is at play.

Important lines that not everyone has
We will now look at some lines that do not appear on all palms.

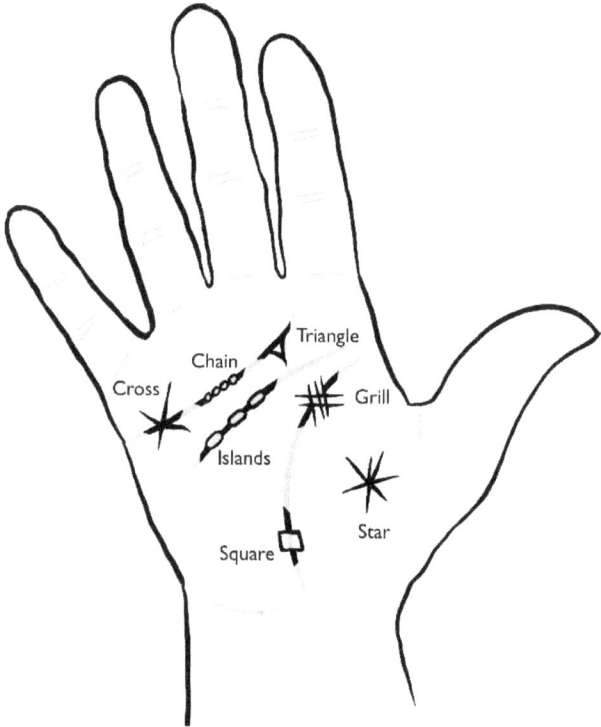

The Fate or Destiny line

Those with this line tend to be luckier than others. They seemingly fall into fortunate situations or make excellent choices. The fate line runs down the hand, usually near the middle from top to bottom. When this line appears on a querent's hand, it may show a determination or goal that will drive or define their lives. There will be a strong passion or success in one specific area.

Stress/strain lines

Long vertical lines at the base of the fingers are called strain lines. These lines can become deeper or lessen depending on the stress in one's life and are a good indicator that a break or respite is needed.

Horizontal lines on the tip or top of the fingers may be indicators of long-term stress which may be a risk to health. These lines may come and go depending upon how you are coping at home or work, but they should not be ignored.

Other lines or shapes on the palm

The major lines discussed above will often have other lines or shapes on them. These marks enable you to add to the information you have already gleaned. The location of various marks is important. For example, if there is a line crossing or marring the life line, it could be something affecting health. It could also be the direction in which a life is heading, such as lifestyle or plans. If the mark is on the head line, then the issue will relate to an intellectual pursuit, be it work or finance. Finally, if the variation is on the heart line, it could be something to do with a relationship or family issue but is sure to be emotional.

Here's a list of significant shapes you may see on palms. These will help you drill down to find out more information for your querent:

- *Chains*. These may mean there will be some obstacle in the area the line appears on.
- *Cross*. This needs to be a proper cross, not just where two lines are meeting. A cross always means there is a change that will need to be made or will be made for you. They are representative of a long-term issue affecting the line they are on but are not necessarily bad as the change may lead to a positive outcome.
- *Grilles.* These are usually negative, and mean effort and energy are scattered. There will be a difficulty in reaching a goal or event. The querent may struggle to address the issue and needs some direction or help to move forward. When found on a life line, ask what goal/dream is not happening?
- *Islands*. Energy is slowed down or scattered. Islands mean a disruption to something that is occurring and affecting you negatively. There may be frustration, anger, or denial involved.
- *Triangles*. These are considered auspicious and lucky. When they are on a line, they enhance the power of that line.
- *Stars*. Stars can be good or bad, depending upon placement on the hand. If alone and not on a line, their location is key.
- *Squares*. When a square is on a major line that has no breaks, it may mean the querent feels trapped or needs to change their situation to grow.

Mounts

The mounts on the hand are the fleshy bumps on the palm and give more depth to reading when considered in association with the information gained from the lines. They are related to, and named for, the planets. Some say there are seven mounts on the hand, others say ten. I prefer to focus on six mounts, omitting Mars:

- *Mount of Jupiter*. Base of index finger. Leadership, organisation, authority.
- *Mount of Saturn*. Base of middle finger. Independence, responsibility, discipline.
- *Mount of Apollo or Sun*. Base of ring finger. Ambition, success, happiness.
- *Mount of Mercury*. Base of little finger. Wisdom, intelligence, energy.
- *Mount of Moon or Luna*. Base of palm near wrist. Creativity, idealism, imagination.
- *Mount of Venus*. Base of the thumb. Love, physicality, emotions.

The firmness and height of each mount determines how much they affect the querent for their specific characteristics. The mounts are categorised as being either raised, balanced, or flat. For example, if you had a firm and defined mount of Jupiter, you would likely have good organisation skills and a preference for order. You would be a good leader who is comfortable with being in authority.

Bringing it all together

Now that we have covered many practical aspects, it's important to acknowledge the intuitive side of palmistry. Try gently holding someone's hand, tracing the lines and features upon it, and be open to receiving intuitive messages. At times you may receive psychic flashes just by looking at a hand (in-person or on a photo) before starting an in-depth analysis. These insights can be just as meaningful as the major lines on a hand.

Don't forget to end a reading in a respectful manner. When I have completed a reading, I remind the querent that nothing is set in stone, all fates are only one path, and they can influence their own future. I usually suggest the querent and reader both wash their hands after a reading (as well as before) and eat something to ground themselves.

If you have enjoyed delving into how to read palms and would like to learn more, I've included some book suggestions in the reference section.

About Scarlet Paige
Scarlet Paige is a child of the Earth. She is a founding member and co-High Priestess of Brisbane's largest and longest running witchcraft group, The Circle Coven.

In her early twenties, Scarlet joined a Brisbane Bayside coven and embraced witchcraft. She has never looked back!

Scarlet is an empath and practitioner of all aspects of the Craft. She is a creator of intricate rituals and spellwork. She is also a reader, healer, artist and author, contributing to Living Witchery Beginner Witch Guide *(published 2021).*

In the mundane world, Scarlet is an educator of young minds, partner, as well as mother of two. She loves to travel and is happiest when in the bush or by the sea.

Divinatory Dreaming

By Kim Fairminer

With the syrupy black of a subtropical night draped over me, the lo-fi buzz of the ceiling fan calls me to wilted sheets. It's good dreaming weather. Dark enough, thanks to the blanket of clouds and a late moon rise, and a smidge too warm to sleep past the realm of recall.

We are dreaming bodies and dreaming bodies are affected by physical stimulus. Our bodies do not make a distinction between physical experiences and dream experiences. Running in your dream will stimulate a raised heart rate. Being startled in your dream will create the same biological patterns as being surprised in your waking life.

Waking life, hmmm… How awake are we? So much of what we do and who we are is beyond our conscious awareness. It is from this subconscious realm that most of our dream material originates.

A dream tells us something we don't already consciously know. A dream asks us to wake up to the psychic unknown, beyond the egoic or physical realm (which is often infuriatingly dense and rather hard to ignore). A dream asks us to wake up to that which our soul yearns to make fully conscious.

Our soul has something to say about our waking lives and dreams are how they get the message through. Every night, we are invited by our soul to listen to the messages it sends us, the love letters, the warnings, the confirmations, the inspiration, the comfort…

We don't have to do anything to make this happen other than go to sleep. Sometimes, for dreaming, just half asleep is even better.

Dreaming is easy
Everybody dreams. It has been so for as long as humans have been humans. Despite what LucidDreamer3000 is trying to sell you, there's no technology involved. You dream just as an ancient Egyptian slave dreamt, just as a child in Victorian England dreamt, just as a fisherman rocking in his boat yesterday dreamt.

You sleep, you dream, and sometimes you remember. I know there are some of you reading this thinking 'well, I don't ever remember my dreams'.

You have and you do. Even if you only ever remember one dream in your whole entire life, that one dream is a portal to the otherworld. While it's always nice to have options, you only need one doorway to move between realms.

So, stop stressing about dream recall and lucid dreaming and hypnogogic states and start thinking about improving the quality of your relationship with the otherworlds. If you're loaded up on blue lotus tea and eye pillows and a pristine dream journal, you've created too much expectation; the inhabitants of the otherworlds are likely to visit someone who is more relaxed.

Don't reach and clamour for messages with desperation. Be receptive. Be curious. Be respectful. Sure, there are things you can do in the waking realm to encourage conscious engagement with dream messages but really, it's about being open and being grateful for whatever you receive.

Opening a channel / Preparing to receive

Ritualising your bedtime routine can enhance your success in receiving answers to your divinatory dream questions. By nature, ritual is repetitive, so make sure the activities you choose to include in your bedtime routine aren't so elaborate that you can't complete them when you're on sleepy autopilot. Choose simple but also meaningful actions to prepare your physical and subtle body to receive and hold the divinatory dream message.

Impurities of all kinds are like static on the line. Stress, an irregular schedule, strong odours, electronics, intoxicants, physical clutter, and/or a psychically disturbed environment could all interrupt a clear connection between your body and the dream world. Depending on your personal circumstances, some habits will be easier to tweak than others.

My daughter often wakes me up in the morning, so waking up slowly and dream journaling in bed isn't practical for me. Instead, I make short dream notes through the night only if I wake up and then share any strange or amusing dreams during the morning household rush hour. It's certainly not a perfect scenario for dream recall or journaling yet I feel blessed to integrate dreaming into my family life. This flow between the dreaming and waking realms is where the real magick happens – and I am open to it happening in unexpectedly domestic ways.

So, purify yourself and your space meaningfully but not fanatically. Remember repetition is key. Perhaps putting away any random items in your bedroom and then having a shower may be all it takes to create a feeling of serenity.

If you want to go a little further than the basics, you could spritz the room with a lightly fragranced psychic cleansing spray. Relaxing oil blends in a roller bottle or botanicals in a pouch tucked under your pillow are another way to release a subtle but evocative scent. Smells communicate directly with our subconscious and when used repetitively over time with the same intent, a particular scent will instantly relax and calm.

Herbal tea before bed is also another lovely way to induce calm and has the potential bonus of a midnight trip to the loo. Those half waking states often carry dream memories. If you are blessed with a message or symbol during the night, quickly jot it down with pen and paper (or as an electronic note in your mobile phone, if you must) because you will not remember in the morning.

Depending on your personal psychospiritual framework, you may also like to incorporate stones, amulets, prayers, sigils, breathing techniques, meditation, or visualisations. Sometimes it's nice to go all out but remember it is repeated, ritualised action which is most likely to bring results.

Even once you've developed a pleasing and sustainable bedtime ritual, you will need to be patient – with yourself and with the dream realm. Dream beings don't always pick up the first call, especially if the number is unfamiliar. This is why building and maintaining a relationship with your divine dreaming intelligence is so valuable. Good friends will pick up and/or return your call. As you get to know them and nurture the relationship through your routine and rituals, they will recognise you and you will recognise them and the whole exchange will become a lot easier.

Dream incubation

Many forms of divination begin with a question. With divination through dreaming, questions are optional. Quite often, you'll receive an answer to a question you haven't (consciously) asked. That said, you can also seek answers to your waking life issues by asking the dreaming world for guidance.

This is called dream incubation and has been done for thousands of years across many cultures. In fact, you've probably already done it unintentionally when you've gone to bed with something on your mind and woken up knowing exactly what to do about it. Dream incubation is a way of entering into conversation with the otherworlds, except rather than opening to whatever spirit deems most important for you right now, you are requesting guidance on a specific topic.

As we've already explored, one's activities before bed (which may include dream props, tea, and even overconsumption of cheese) can help open the channel to the dreamworld but any items used during such rituals are not a substitute for quality time spent with the divine intelligence and their symbols. Incorporate physical items as part of your dream offerings and rituals but don't mistake them as the source of the wisdom.

Think of what you can offer, rather than what you will receive, and then be open to receiving anyway.

Your offering may correspond to the nature of your question or a specific being you wish to connect with via your dream. If you are seeking guidance on how to find a new job, you may wish to offer a gold coin. If you are seeking to connect with a crossed-over loved one, you could print a photo of the person. If you want inspiration for an important piece of writing, you might like to offer a feather or an acorn. Follow your intuition.

I like to use a special bowl for offerings beside my bed. If I am seeking guidance on a specific matter, I will write down the question or draw the situation I need help with. Then I sleep and wait. Usually, I allow three nights. Sometimes, I receive a dream message; sometimes, the material situation resolves itself without an answer from the spiritual world *as far as I am consciously aware.*

Just because you don't remember, doesn't mean nothing happened. Appreciate the mystery.

I remembered my dream. Now what?
Congratulations on remembering your dream. Or part of your dream. Even if all you can remember from your overnight adventure is a few words from an annoying advertising jingle or something about a bobby pin. Even if you aren't even sure whether it was something from a dream or just something your under-caffeinated brain tossed to you in protest, be grateful for whatever titbits you receive. Be curious about it and work with it.

Now that you've successfully consciously connected the dream world to your waking world (however tenuous) do something to reinforce and strengthen that connection. Anchor your dream message in the waking world by creating additional psychic landing space. There are several ways to do this:

- Amplify the dream symbols and look for common themes (as discussed further on)
- Create art inspired by the dream (this art is a portal between realms)
- Interact with the dream symbols/themes when you come across them in your waking life
- Re-enter the dream through meditation and ask a key character or symbol questions (write down the question, enter a light trance, connect with your focal point, and record the response)
- Re-enter the dream and explore the landscape or visit a similar landscape in the material realm.

When you do these activities, you are intentionally thinning the veil between the material realm and the otherworlds. You are open and receptive and become the vessel for additional messages. You are the portal – like a letter box for flyers from the soul. Watch for spontaneous insights and, if they come, accept them with gratitude.

Much of this is process, not outcome. Dreaming is limitless and has no outcome, no end, only a deepening into mystery.

A bobby pin

Why a bobby pin? You can roll this over in your mind while you have your coffee. There is no hurry. Hurrying is death to dreamland. As are alarm clocks. Slow down and wonder.

Bobby pins are surprisingly interesting when you stop to ponder them. They're the sort of thing one completely overlooks, until you absolutely need one. And often you don't need it for your hair. I've used one in place of a paperclip before and to poke something inside of a hole in the hope of performing a miraculous fix. I guess that's what it's supposed to do for one's hair. Prop it up, resolve the problem, bring the world and one's crowning glory back into alignment. Bobby pins hold things together.

You might like to draw a bobby pin. Dreams love to be drawn. Even dubious fragments of possible dreams love to be drawn. It makes the otherworld feel seen. The beings of the otherworld love that as much as humans do.

You continue to go about your day. At some seemingly random point during that very usual day, you come across a bobby pin – on your table at the café, on the window ledge in the bus, down the side of the couch that you had the inexplicable urge to clean. It could be anywhere.

Your egoic mind tells you it's just a coincidence; confirmation bias happens all the time. Deeper within, a little further down and into your body, around your heart centre or in your belly, there's a feeling. A connection is made with something other, something both within and beyond yourself.

You didn't find the bobby pin; the bobby pin found you. It is a message from the otherworld.

You've now noticed the psychic thread, which manifested in your waking life in the form of a bobby pin. Will you pick it up and follow it?

What were you thinking about at the time you happened upon that random bobby pin? A delicate conversation with a loved one? The job application you sent yesterday? The monumental mess in the kitchen waiting for you?

What is calling out to be brought together in your waking life? Where can you apply a simple fix to bring order?

Divination by dreaming isn't passive. Yes, you need to be at least half asleep or in an altered state of awareness to receive the initial message, but your conscious mind needs to be open, receptive, and awake to truly hear.

You don't find the meaning of dreams in dream dictionaries.

You need to follow the thread. It's your thread, your mystery to solve.

Conversing with the divine

Let's unpack what happened there in a little more detail. The symbol, in this case a lone bobby pin, though of uncertain origin, came from the spirit world. To you. For a reason. To unearth that reason, you first must pay attention to the symbol. You must recognise the arrival of the messenger and receive delivery of the message. You must revere the innate divinity of the symbol.

It helps to anchor the symbol in the material realm – by writing it down, by drawing it, by telling someone about it. In this way, you enter a conversation with the symbol. Perhaps sacred dialogue is a better word? Much as you communicate with divine intelligence via cards or runes or planets, the dream and its symbol/s are your connection to the divine.

Together, you and the divine intelligence flesh out the possible meanings of the symbol. Notice, I didn't say *the* meaning of the symbol. Symbols, by their very nature, are multifaceted; they mean different things at different times in different contexts to different people. You need to have your own conversation with and through this symbol to find out what it means for you today.

Dream amplification

Dream amplification, often used by Jungian psychotherapists, can be used to expand the symbol with all the extra information we know about it. To follow the metaphor of sound, it's tuning in to the frequency of the symbol and turning the volume up.

While we casually amplified the symbol of the bobby pin earlier, it often helps to draw and label the symbol in the centre of a page and then write ideas and concepts associated with that symbol all around it.

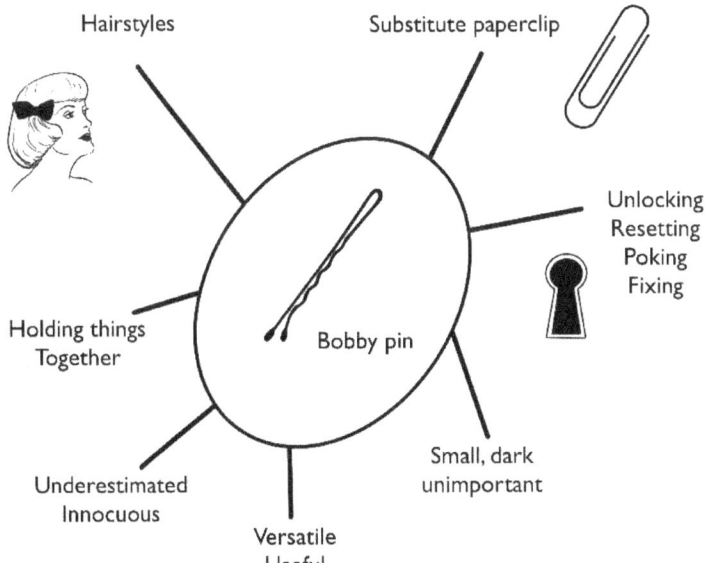

This process works as well with non-tangible symbols (e.g. darkness) as it does with living creatures (e.g. black cat) and non-animate objects (e.g. a pen). Include collective cultural associations as well as personal associations and memories. For example, a black cat is often considered 'unlucky' but you may have fond memories of a family pet. Both meanings are relevant and should be included in your exploration of the symbol.

Amplifying each symbol in a single dream or a series of dreams will help you see an over-arching theme and pin down the core message. The dreams you have in one night are usually presenting the same soul message to you in a variety of forms to help you understand. Like the cries of a hungry baby, messages from the soul are simultaneously incoherent, persistent, and visceral.

If I was to connect the three symbols mentioned above – darkness, a black cat, a pen – I see overlapping themes of blackness, shadow, inky and shape-shifting creativity. Perhaps supressed or hidden ideas are ready to emerge?

You already have the plot or narrative from your dream, you just need to think in symbolic rather than literal terms to understand the divinatory message. This is a valuable, indeed essential skill for diviners of all persuasions. Once you become practiced in reading in non-literal/intuitive ways, understanding your dreams is a lot easier (as well as your card readings, tea leaf readings etc.).

You can't look up or directly translate a dream; you can be open and tend to them. Over time, you will attune to the symbolic dialect of your own psyche.

Big dreams and little dreams

Yes, dreams can be prophetic, but what's a prophecy without the ability to change the outcome? Dreams tell you what you don't already know. Dreams wake you up to something you are oblivious to in your waking life and it's usually something important. Important things require action.

Don't let your ego get in the way of acting. Having prophetic dreams and then saying 'I told you so' isn't all that admirable, at least not repeatedly. Sometimes we cannot change things. Sometimes we can.

Don't mistake the ease and simplicity of dreaming as a license to be passive. Yes, receptivity welcomes the initial messages into your consciousness but receiving those messages carries a responsibility to yourself, and sometimes to those around you, to respond with awareness.

Not every dream is a big dream, but you know a big dream when you have one. You wake up changed. The feeling stays with you. At the same time, stay anchored to the Earth and your waking life. (This is the path of the witch – to walk with a foot in each realm.)

Ignore a big dream at your peril. You received this important message for a reason: You have the power to create change.

Regular dreams are also gifts.

You don't need to do dreamwork/dreamplay every day – although, of course, you certainly can and with great benefit to all dimensions of personal and spiritual life. Sometimes simply sharing the highlights of your dream with your family, housemate, or a friend is all the acknowledgement needed or is practical at the time.

Dreams can be incredibly humorous too, so laugh.

While writing this chapter, I dreamt of doing a load of laundry in the toilet with dishwashing liquid. There's a whole lot to unpack there about cleanliness and waste and domesticity but it's also funny. At its simplest, maybe I need to lighten up about my household chores?

Humour is one of the ways dreams grab our attention and I won't be forgetting this dream in a hurry. The emotional content of dreams is always important. Being terrified, or aroused, or joyful are also common ways dreams grab and hold your attention.

Always notice the mood of the dream and how it flows. If you are afraid and running in your dream, something needs to shift in the dreamscape to either stop the running or stop the fear. The pace and direction of the dream energy usually flows in a particular direction until something intervenes to redirect that energetic flow. If you are having nightmares or a recurring dream, something needs to change for the distressing dream to stop.

Divination, including dreaming, is an invitation for you to expand your awareness of prevailing influences, including the probable trajectory based on past and current actions. It empowers you with foresight and gives you the opportunity to (re)direct the likely course of events.

As you take in the nocturnal sounds and scents in your bedroom tonight, you enter the liminal realm between waking and dreaming. As your eyelids grow heavy and close, you are poised to connect with the limitless wisdom of the otherworlds. Dream well.

About Kim Fairminer

Kim is an astrologer, writer, and witch with more than 20 years hands-on experience as a magical practitioner. She has been a member of The Circle Coven for over ten years, including six years in the role of High Priestess. Before her life-changing midlife transits, she was an editor for a multinational company. She is author and co-editor of Living Witchery: Beginner Witch Guide *(published in 2021), writes horoscopes and forecasts for a range of publications, and shares esoteric wisdom in her online community. Kim writes, stargazes, and circle-casts from her home in suburban Brisbane.*

You can learn more about her work at kimfairminer.com

Folk Magic and the Art of Divination in Everyday Life

By Scarlet Paige

Folk magic is often described as low or practical magic; however, I define it as everyday divination methods used to predict, control, or influence the world around us. So, you ask excitedly, how does folk magic fit into divination?

Throughout history and across cultures, people have formed relationships with each other, with animals, with places, plants, and objects. These relationships are often mutually beneficial and dynamic. As our world continues to change and grow, the types of items used for folk magic and divination also changes.

By taking the suffix 'mancy' (meaning divination) and adding it to the end of a word, it explains the form of divination you are using. For example, there is the little known and rarely consulted art of tyromancy, which is divination using cheese, to the hugely popular tarotmancy which is divination using Tarot cards.

Folk magic divination is often simple. If you need advice, you can request (or pray) for a sign or symbol which is apparent in the seen (and heard) world and then interpret the meanings. There are standard meanings you can use when interpreting a sign. However, it is important to also consider your own experience with the animal/insect/plant/thing/item that you are seeing or interacting with. Also, you should reflect on how the item is responding to you.

Look within yourself and your relationship with the item. Is your experience one of fear or reverence, happiness or concern? For example, if you see an animal, do you feel a kinship with it? Do you have a personal relationship with it?

You can ask to be shown a sign in any way you like. For example, make a simple statement or just ask a question in your mind or under your breath. Be reverent and dramatic if that is what you prefer. Any simple statement will work. I like to say:

Beloved Universe, I ask for your help and guidance. Send me a sign about…

Once you have asked for a sign, be observant. Take note of the world around you. Perhaps the sign will come in the form of the next insect you see or the words you overhear. It might even be a literal street sign.

Let's look at the various signs which await you.

Ailuromancy (cats)
In ancient Egypt, the cat was seen as a sacred and magical animal which was honoured as a vessel for the Goddess herself. Keeping a cat was seen as good luck, as cats were not owned but came and went as they pleased, roaming freely. A fascination with cats has continued through the years, with the role of cats in folk magic being no exception.

A black cat crossing your path is considered either bad or good luck depending upon your circumstances and upbringing. Seeing a cat sneezing indicates luck is on the way and having a cat fall asleep on your lap is thought to bless you with good fortune. Divinatory messages can also be received while observing the sleeping positions and places of cats, as well as the length of time that they slumber.

Other folk divinatory meanings associated with cats are:

- ✦ If you wish to see someone who has been absent, rub your hands up a cat's back against the fur as you say the person's name nine times. (This may be particularly effective if the person you wish to see is a doctor as the cat will likely protest at the rough treatment.)
- ✦ If a cat wishes to go outside, it means the weather is about to change.
- ✦ A cat meowing means visitors are due.
- ✦ If you are looking for a lost item, tell the cat what you are looking for and then follow the direction of the cat's paws when it lays down.

Apples or pears
Apples have long held a place in folk magic, as they are inexpensive and easy to source. Bobbing for apples used to be a way for a young woman to find out the name of her future suitor. The local boys' names would be written on each apple and the girls would bob for them. A similar activity was to peel an apple in one long strand, then drop the peel onto the ground looking to form an initial.

Arachnomancy (spiders)
Divination from the appearance and behaviour of spiders includes ascribing meanings to how many legs they have. Arachnomancy is so popular that there are now apps and websites dedicated to this divination method which has well and truly entered the 21st century.

- The shape, size and location of spider webs also have divinatory meanings.
- Seeing a spider with lost legs can be a message about one's health and to have it checked. The fewer legs, the more serious the message.
- Spider webs represent home and family and seeing a spider living in a web in your home is lucky.
- Walking into a web can mean a message to watch over one's family and keep them close.

Alectryomancy (chickens and roosters)
There are divination meanings associated with the eating patterns of chickens, specifically a black or white rooster. This method of divination can be used in many ways, though is not so practical if you live in an inner-city apartment.

- Create a spirit board (or area on the ground) with YES, NO, or various choices of answers. Throw a handful of grain or corn onto the area and then release a rooster in the middle to peck at the grain. The rooster's movements can then be read as needed. For example, if all the grain on NO is pecked up first, there's some helpful guidance for you.
- A rooster crowing and waking you up is a good omen.
- A rooster sitting on your fence or house is a sign of good luck.

Batrachomancy (frogs)
Frogs are a symbol of the Egyptian goddess Heqet who is linked to rebirth and transformation. They can be used for divination by observing the height of their hopping. Frogs are also signs of weather, fertility, romance, and love.

- Hearing the croaking of frogs is an indicator of rain coming.
- Seeing or hearing a frog means a change is coming in the weather or in oneself.
- A frog may be a symbol of upcoming romance and/or pregnancy.
- Frogs are symbols of new beginnings, if you are starting a new endeavour of any kind, seeing a frog is a good omen.

Ceromancy (wax)
Choose a candle of the colour associated with your question (there's a helpful list in *Living Witchery Beginner Witch Guide*). If you are unsure, use a white candle. As you light the candle, ask your question aloud. Take a moment to focus on the candle as the wick burns. Once it is well alight, tip the candle and allow the wax to drip onto your chosen surface. If you are using water, use a shallow bowl and look for shapes forming in the water. If you are using a flat surface, close your eyes as the wax drips and hold the candle in one area. Once you

feel you have enough wax to make a prediction, put out the candle and begin looking for symbols, shapes, numbers, letters, or something relevant to the question you have asked.

Coins, rings, and food

In Europe, items such as coins and simple metal rings were often baked into pies, bread, cakes, or even put into mashed foods and stews. At engagements and marriages, symbolic rings baked into celebratory foods were said to predict who would be next to marry. At end-of-year celebrations and other special events, coins were a lucky find. If you found a coin, it meant good fortune for the future. Unless, of course, if you accidently bit the coin and broke a tooth. Then it meant a trip to the dentist.

> If you are attending a wedding, take an extra piece of cake home with you. Place it in a white cotton cloth tied with a ribbon or cord and sleep on it that night. You may dream of the person you will marry or end up with.

Entomomancy (insects)

There are too many insects to delve into them all in this chapter, but here are some common ones to get you started. It is important to note that the symbolic meanings vary across countries and cultures. You must also consider your personal interpretations of the insect in relation to meaning.

- *Ants*: These tiny insects have varied meanings, and their colour and number can also change the interpretation. They are seen as both good and bad luck depending upon your culture. A general meaning is that reward for hard work is coming, be it luck, money, or travel.
- *Bees*: Busy bees are symbols of fertility and progression of a task. They can be a reminder of what needs to be done, or of the finalisation of a task. Bees can be celebratory or a warning.
- *Butterflies* or *Cicadas*: Transformation. Birth, death, and rebirth. Time for taking stock of what is, has been and will be.
- *Dragonflies*: These fleeting animals are a symbol of happiness, luck, and protection.
- *Grasshoppers*: Money. Courage. Take a chance.
- *Ladybug*: Luck and a happy home. Visitors are coming.
- *Moth*: Symbol of endings and, at times, the death of someone close to you.
- *Praying Mantis*: A time to pause and take stock. Don't make any quick decisions.

> In old Celtic lore, there is a link between this world and the next. When a person wants to get a message to someone who has died, they talk to the bees. In some places, this transitioned into telling the bees when someone was born or married as well. It was believed that if you did not keep the bees informed, they would fly away and not return, taking their sweet honey with them.

Oenomancy (wine)

Oenomancy is a fun way to have a few drinks and predict the future. The patterns left in the bottom of a wine glass can be read in the same way as they are read in tea. You can also choose to spill/dribble wine onto a white cloth asking a question to be answered and look for patterns.

> If someone is given a tea or coffee with a spoon in it and they do not remove the spoon prior to taking their first sip, pregnancy is potentially looming for someone close to the person drinking the hot beverage.

Oomancy (eggs)

Eggs are a symbol of fertility and growth and have long been used in various divinatory practices. With a single raw egg, you can perform a simple divination process. Make a hole at the top and the bottom. Ask your question then blow the contents into a clear glass or bowl. Ensure the hole is big enough to do this. Look at the egg contents from all sides, search for shapes, letters, or numbers.

The humble egg is said to be able to make you feel better. If you wish to be rid of something, perhaps a pain or illness, rub the egg in a circular motion on the area where you feel pain and in a loud voice demand that the pain/illness is to leave you and enter the egg. Once you have covered the area well with the rolling of the egg, bury the egg during the dark moon, being careful not to break it. Once the egg is fully covered by earth, stomp on the ground saying, "I release you!" The Earth will absorb and transform the bad energy.

Ophiomancy (snakes)

In Australia, we have many snakes not found anywhere else in the world. Snakes bring transition and change. Shedding one's skin for a new one can prophesise a romantic and adventurous idea, though this is something snakes routinely do as they grow.

- ✦ Seeing a snake may be an omen of an upcoming life change.

- ✦ Finding a snakeskin means a change has already begun and is inevitable.
- ✦ Those who have strong links to Christianity may see the snake as a symbol of deceit, a bad omen, or portend the breakup of a relationship. This relates to the story of Adam, Eve, and the sinister snake in the Garden of Eden.

Ornithomancy (birds)

The various types of birds, their locations, seeing, hearing, being attacked by a bird (hello, magpie season) or finding a dead one have meanings. The location of the bird can be important. If a bird is seen to be happy and flying free, it is usually a good omen. If birds are seen flocking in one location, it can be a bad omen.

- ✦ Birds around or in the home, flying into a window, entering the home, or finding a dead bird in your yard are all indications that bad luck will arrive soon.
- ✦ It is good luck for a bird to poop on you. You may like to buy a lottery ticket.
- ✦ Hitting a bird with your car or being chased by a bird is not a good sign. Things are about to get bumpy.
- ✦ Keeping a peacock feather in your home in Westernised cultures is considered bad luck. However, in some Eastern traditions, it's the opposite. It's all about location, location, location.
- ✦ An albatross is considered good luck to sailors (if not harmed). Finding a dead albatross before a journey was a symbol of death and failure of a journey.
- ✦ Black birds, such as crows and ravens, are usually considered bad luck when seen in flocks. However, in London, ravens are considered lucky when seen around the Tower of London.

Stichomancy (books)

Historically, only the rich had access to books and were able to read, though that is not as true today. Bibliomancy is using the bible for divination and rhapsodomancy refers to using a poetry book. There are many ways to use books for divination but here is a simple method:

1. Firstly, choose a book.
2. Close your eyes and ask a question aloud.
3. Now open the book to a random page.
4. On that page, run your finger down until you feel the need to stop.
5. Open your eyes and read out that sentence.
6. Apply the sentence to your question.

Elemental divination – Water, Air, Earth, Fire
Aeromancy (Air)
The element of Air can be found in wind, rainbows, clouds, and storms. Bells, wind vanes, ribbons, flags, and other objects can send messages from the spiritual realm to the mundane world.

- *Aeromancy*: Divination of changing atmospheric conditions.
- *Austromancy*: Forms of aeromancy which use the direction and strength of the wind for divination purposes.
- *Ceraunoscopy*: Observing the frequency and length of thunder and lightning for hidden meanings.
- *Metormancy*: Divination through the observation of meteors, comets, and shooting stars.
- *Nephomancy*: Observation of patterns and shapes formed by clouds.

Geomancy (Earth)
Divination of the element of Earth may include observing your environment for various landforms. It can also be observing rocks, crystals, soil, and sand. For thousands of years, stones or small items have been collected and drawn out of bags (and sometimes cast upon the ground) to provide answers to questions.

- *Runes*: Stone or crystal which have been marked in some way with words or symbols. When casting runes, throw gently in an arc, the ones closest to you and face up are more relevant.
- *Geomancy*: The study of natural markings and lines on the ground.
- *Lithomancy*: Using precious stones by casting them and observing patterns and designs.
- *Hag stones*: These lovely stones, also called witch or adder stones, are usually found near fresh or salt water as the hole is often made by water/decayed plant erosion through the stone. The hole must be naturally occurring and go all the way through the rock, from one side to the other.

  Traditionally, the stone must be found by the owner, not bought, nor given as a gift. You can wish on a hag stone by holding it in your left hand whilst rubbing it with your left thumb and saying your wish over and over. They can be used as protection stones by attaching them to that which you need to protect. When looking through a hag stone, it is said that you may see the truth and/or fae and otherworldly creatures in their true appearance.

Hydromancy (Water)

Water is necessary for all life and is a cleansing and renewing element. Water (be it salt or fresh) can be used to banish and cleanse items as well as for scrying. Any liquid, oil for example, can be used for hydromancy if preferred.

- *Dowsing*: A method of divination to find lost or unknown things located underground (such as a water source or missing item).
- *Hydromancy*: Scrying into water or noting tidal variations.
- *Lecanomancy*: Using a basin of water for scrying into.
- *Pegomancy*: A form of hydromancy using a sacred pool or spring.

> Legend has it that if you visit Rome and throw a single coin into the Trevi fountain, your return is ensured. For this to work you must use your right hand and toss the coin over your left shoulder.

Pyromancy (Fire)

Fire is considered the ultimate cleanser and has long been used for divination. Tribes and cultural groups used fire not only for warmth and cooking but to also help make decisions for the future. As items were ritually burnt, the smoke shapes, sounds, sparks, coals, and flames were read. Once the fire died down, the ash itself was observed for shapes, or markings.

- *Botanomancy*: A form of pyromancy which involves burning various types of trees, leaves, and branches.
- *Causinomancy*: Objects are cast into a fire and their burning patterns are observed.
- *Pyroscopy*: Burning a sheet of paper on a white surface and examining the resulting stains.
- *Lampadomancy*: Using an oil lamp flame or torch flame.
- *Libanomancy*: Burning incense and reading the smoke and ash.

Trance

Divination using objects is quite simple, as you use your senses to interpret the world around you through your eyes, ears, hands or even smell. But when you wish to take this further, look not outside but inside yourself using trance and meditation. These methods of internal divination are more difficult to begin with but can provide great insights.

- *Metagnomy*: Seeing future events in a hypnotic trance.
- *Necromancy*: Contacting spirits using a Ouija board or other method.
- *Oneiromancy*: Using dreams to determine the future.

And there you have it. A chapter that incorporates divination with some aspects of folk magick. If you love folk magick and you love divination, let this information inspire you to bring magick into your every day.

About Scarlet Paige

Scarlet Paige is a child of the Earth. She is a founding member and co-High Priestess of Brisbane's largest and longest running witchcraft group, The Circle Coven.

In her early twenties, Scarlet joined a Brisbane Bayside coven and embraced witchcraft. She has never looked back!

Scarlet is an empath and practitioner of all aspects of the Craft. She is a creator of intricate rituals and spellwork. She is also a reader, healer, artist and author, contributing to Living Witchery Beginner Witch Guide *(published 2021).*

In the mundane world, Scarlet is an educator of young minds, partner, as well as mother of two. She loves to travel and is happiest when in the bush or by the sea.

FOCUS: Cards

Although cards don't have the same long history as some other forms of divination, they are one of the most popular forms of contemporary divination tools.

Cartomancy

By Sandra Lee

The humble pack of playing cards has long been used as a safe and stealthy way to divine the future without drawing unwanted attention from religious leaders or nosey neighbours. It is not too dramatic to say that until recently, such things could lead to being outcast from one's home and society, punishable by imprisonment, or death. Here, I will share what I know of the divine art of cartomancy, including my interpretations, compiled from decades of practice, research, and lived experience. I hope you enjoy this chapter as heartily as the Jack of Hearts.

My earliest experiences of divining with playing cards were sitting around my grandparent's kitchen table as a child, or in the hallway to catch the afternoon breeze on a hot summer evening. In those pre-internet and three-channels-on-TV days, my very patient Nan and Pa would teach us grandkids how to play pontoon, poker, gin rummy and canasta. (When we were too excited or unruly, they taught us solitaire. In hindsight, this was the nicest way to give us a gentle time out.) Nan would comment on the cards we were dealt or played, almost as an aside while we were playing. Sometimes we would ask her to tell us more. Mostly, we would be too busy arguing about who was winning by counting and recounting the matchsticks we had in our piles.

In my teens, my interest in cartomancy was stoked again. This time, it was by a local psychic my Ma used to visit named Frances Bevan. His book *Your Future by Reading Playing Cards* was available at my local library way back in the 1990s. My sister and I devoured this book and any others we could find, spending hours at my kitchen table, shuffling, deciphering and writing notes on this mysterious and deceptively simple form of seeing into our future. So many notes, handwritten into beautiful notebooks which we still have to this day (although they are rather ratty looking now). And the things we used to obsess over – good heavens!

I still consider shuffling, cutting the deck and taking notes to be the very best way to learn the art of cartomancy. Over coffee, or tea, with eyes full of tears or hearts filled with desire. After all these years, my love of cartomancy has not subsided, and it is still my go-to form of divination.

One of the delights of cartomancy is the easy availability of playing cards. Most households have at least one deck of cards lying around, or they can be purchased rather cheaply from newsagents, service stations, discount stores and grocery shops.

The basics

Cards	Correspondences
52 cards	52 weeks in the year
13 cards in a suit	13 lunar months each year
12 court cards	12 months of the years; 12 zodiac signs
4 suits	4 seasons each year; 4 periods in each day; 4 stages of life
Hearts	Cups – 'my cup is full'
Spades	Swords – 'prickly situations'
Diamonds	Coins – 'that which holds value'
Clubs	Saplings – 'new growth takes work'

Quirky traditions

I've dabbled in Tarot and Lenormand but I always return to cartomancy, which is plain and simple card reading. There are many other traditions and reading styles you can add to your divination toolbox. Some are quaint and quirky; others are just peculiar. Using your nous and doing what feels right is always recommended. Here are some of the 'must-dos' I've come across:

- ✦ Cards should be wrapped in black or red silk only.
- ✦ Cards should be kept on the highest shelf to raise their frequency to be above the matters of the world.
- ✦ Sleep with a new deck of cards under your pillow before removing them from the box for use in divination.
- ✦ Cards should only be cut using the left hand, towards the reader.
- ✦ Cards should only be shuffled by the reader, not the querent. The querent then selects cards once they are spread across the table by the reader.
- ✦ The first pack of cartomancy cards must be gifted to the reader, never purchased. This 'tradition' is also common in Tarot communities.

I no longer follow these traditions, with the exceptions of sleeping with new decks under my pillow and cutting with my left hand, which is more muscle memory than conscious decision these days. I wholeheartedly recommend listening to the cards for guidance. In addition, I also ask my cards to tell me about themselves on the first shuffle and spread that I do.

Starting out

Studying the cards by doing readings for yourself is the best way to learn cartomancy. There are general and time-honoured meanings, interpretations, and guides to follow, and these are an important part of your journey into learning cartomancy.

- Begin by learning the meaning of the cards by colour, suit, number, and court card significations.
- Use small one- or three-card spreads. As you become more confident, the larger spreads may appeal.
- Take plenty of notes of your first impressions of the cards, then come back to the reading in a week, a month, a year and add more notes about the situation.
- Notetaking is essential, as is following up. Document the date and vibe of the reading.
- Be patient. Like any new technique, time is the key to successful interpretation.
- Take your time and try being in the moment, if not relaxed. A frisson of excitement and emotion is normal, as most people do not turn to divination when their life is calm and bountiful.

Choosing your deck

Finding a deck that works for you is easy – you will no doubt start with what is on hand. New decks may call to you from time to time, but any deck that feels good in your hands will suffice. Playing cards are generally the same size (57–64 mm x 89 mm) around the world, lightweight and easy to hold and shuffle. The most popular materials for playing cards are plastic, vinyl, and paper. In my personal experience, plastic is most durable, vinyl can get sticky after many uses, while paper ages the fastest. My favourite deck is made from a cotton-paper blend and, while it is showing its age, it has held up well over the decades.

Shuffling and cutting the cards

When reading for yourself, the shuffle is a natural process. Still your mind, focus on your question and intuitively stop. Traditionally, the cards are cut. This means separating the deck into three piles with the left hand, working to the left. Then place the cards back into one pile and pull the cards to be read from the top of the deck.

When reading cards for others in-person, you shuffle the deck while the querent discusses the question on their mind. Then put the cards on the table and ask the querent to pick them up and shuffle the deck again, while thinking of their query. The querent then cuts the deck into three piles to the left, using their left hand, before placing the cards back into one pile. You (as reader) then pull the required cards from the top of the deck for the chosen spread.

Jumpers or dropped cards
Any cards which jump out or drop from the deck while shuffling should be noted and reinserted into the deck. These cards indicate unexpected or surprising events that occur quickly and hold significance in the reading. If they are court cards, they may represent people who are relevant to the querent in some way.

Reversed cards
Most modern decks of cards are designed to be read with no distinct right or wrong way up.

Over the years, I have swung between using reversed cards and only upright cards, depending on my mood and most current research. I gain just as much insight and knowledge by sticking to upright cards and using larger spreads to gain more information. I highly recommend all newcomers to the art of cartomancy start off using only upright card interpretations. Once you get your head around the basics of the practice, you can then experiment with your methodology using reversed meanings if desired. Putting the pieces together in even a small spread can be quite overwhelming in the beginning. Keeping it simple is a perfect starting place.

Card magick
One of my favourite things in the world is discovering old decks of playing cards in charity shops. The older and more worn, the better! I write messages on the cards to gift to loved ones, sending them a little magick wrapped in love. I use old cards as bookmarks or pop them into my phone cover to remind me of rituals, affirmations, or manifestations I am working on.

If the deck particularly resonates with me, I will use certain cards in my spell work and rituals. This can be as easy as selecting the corresponding cards to boost the impact of your ritual. A more complicated option is to draw cards from start to finish throughout your ritual process and use the cards to guide your magick through to completion. Do this by following the basic correspondences of the suits, and breaking the meanings down by number (e.g. Ace for beginnings, 2 for couples).

A ritual setting is sometimes integral to the card reading itself, particularly for yearly spreads and when major decisions are required.

Selecting your spread

There are many spreads in cartomancy, all used for the same purpose – to predict the outcome of an event. I prefer to keep my daily and weekly draws simple, such as one card a day to catch the vibe and a three-card draw for my week-ahead reading. I also do a 12-card spread at the start of each lunar new year, one card per month, and a 13-card spread on my solar return each year. It is always fascinating to look back over your notes and see just how accurate the cards always are.

A word to the wise: it can also be a tad scary, particularly when you are new to cartomancy, when you draw a lot of Spades, so try being in a resilient and grounded frame of mind before you draw.

Year ahead or wheel of the year spread

The year ahead spread works best on significant dates such as the new year, both lunar and Gregorian. The wheel of the year spread works best when done on your birthday.

Shuffle, cut and draw 12 cards, to symbolise the 12 months of the year ahead. Draw another card and place in the middle. This card will show the overall 'flavour' of the year ahead.

Simple seven spread

This is a simple layout which is ideal for a specific query. It is less suitable for a general reading. After shuffling and cutting, seven cards are laid out in an inverted V from left to right.

Position	Meaning
1st card	Home and domestic issues
2nd card	Current influences, factors directly related to present circumstances
3rd card	Relationships, love, friends, business, rivals, or enemies
4th card	What the enquirer hopes will happen
5th card	Assistance or obstacles that will help or hinder
6th card	Events that will affect the immediate future
7th card	Helpful influences or fortunate circumstances.

Yes/no spread

The quickest way to get a yes or no answer from the cards is to shuffle the deck while pondering your question. Cut and stack the deck and select the first card.

- *Hearts* = yes
- *Diamonds* = yes but you will need to use your resources to make it happen
- *Clubs* = yes but it will require hard work
- *Spades* = no.

Wish cards

When you already have an outcome in mind and need to know whether your wish will come true, use this spread to find your answer fast. Searching for the wish card is a good alternative to a yes/no spread.

With your wish in mind, shuffle and cut the cards. Starting from the bottom of the deck, picture side up, look through the shuffled and stacked deck until you come to the 9 of Hearts. If the cards on either side of it are red, your wish will come true; if the cards on either side are black, your wish will be denied.

Choosing a significator

The 12 court cards correlate to the colouring and personality of the querent. Traditionally, the court cards have signified the gender of the querent, though over many years of reading cards, I have often found this to be inaccurate.
I prefer to use the following significations:

- *Kings* represent either gender, indicating more dominant personalities and what are considered traditionally as masculine traits.
- *Queens* represent either gender, indicating more passive, nurturing personalities and what are considered traditionally as feminine traits.
- *Jacks* represent either gender, indicating young people, but also more youthful, naïve, or immature personalities and what are considered childlike traits.

It is not unusual to find people in their elder years appear as a Jack if they are young at heart or are behaving in an immature way regarding their query. Choosing a significator is often unnecessary in a personal reading, as the court cards can signify your mood or the traits you need to embody to get the results desired. For example, if you have pale blue eyes, red hair and a fair complexion, yet you keep coming up in a reading as the King of Spades, this could be indicative of your current mood (dark, solemn) or the traits you need to embody to get results (authoritative).

When conducting readings for other people, significators are useful to discern who is who in someone else's world. Although family members may all have the same colouring, the court cards will reveal the personality traits of each person shown in a reading:

- *Hearts*: Hazel eyes; fair to medium hair; fair complexion. Loving, nurturing, generous, emotional.
- *Clubs*: Brown eyes; dark hair; ruddy complexion. Hardworking, business oriented, enthusiastic, may struggle to finish what is started.
- *Diamonds*: Blue, grey, or light green eyes; blonde, grey, or red hair; pale complexion. Discreet, money-minded, flinty, hard to know.
- *Spades*: Dark eyes; dark to black hair; dark complexion. Sullen, distant, solemn, authoritative.

Card interpretations

There are an extensive variety of resources available to define the meaning of each card in cartomancy. I've been 'playing with the cards' for over two decades now and will still devour any book, article, or web page that crosses my path for more information on this most practical form of divination. Getting the cards to talk to you and tell you the story within them is the pearl we seek, but we all must start at the beginning, and here are my interpretations of the cards. Learning the art of cartomancy starts here.

Enjoy!

Card	Meanings
Aces	Messages, news, and beginnings. A new cycle or fresh attitude arrives, but Aces alone do not guarantee success. The single pip represents the self and the desire for action.
Ace of Hearts	The home. Good news. Messages of love. The beginning of something you love.
Ace of Diamonds	Erratic good luck. An unexpected event. An energetic beginning to a course of action.
Ace of Clubs	News that may bring a temporary boost in income. Letters, paperwork, documents.
Ace of Spades	New and exciting adventures. A fresh start with uncertain outcomes. Taking a chance with no guarantee of success.

Card	Meanings
Twos	Conversations, discussions, exchange of ideas, words, and opinions. Partnerships, either coming together or pulling apart. Dual pips show duelling situations.
Two of Hearts	Celebrations. Happy events. Loving partnerships.
Two of Diamonds	Sharp words, disagreements about finances. Small increases in money.
Two of Clubs	Unnecessary worries and disputes. Small pressures and strains.
Two of Spades	Moving forward. Idea and aspirations beginning to take concrete form. A hopeful start.
Threes	Expansion on a small level, growth, opportunities that will disappear if not grasped with a firm hand. Ideas and new horizons.
Three of Hearts	Friends, sociable encounters. Passionate words spoken in the heat of the moment.
Three of Diamonds	Good luck through the cooperation and help of friends and associates.
Three of Clubs	Slowness, sluggishness, inertia. Events moving slowly. Irritating and unhelpful intervention of others in matters that do not concern them.
Three of Spades	A frustrating meeting or conversation. Speaking your mind. Prudent and careful consideration of plans.
Fours	Steadiness, focus, a practical approach. Staying within the boundaries, for better or for worse. Boxed in or a comfortable place. Four pips show borders.
Four of Hearts	Solid emotional relationships. Love and friendships that endure. Small commitments.
Four of Diamonds	Established success, steady good fortune. Things going so well there is a danger of complacency.
Four of Clubs	Financial success and prosperity. A stroke of unexpected good luck. Help offered at just the right time.
Four of Spades	Solid progress in putting an idea into effect. Good luck and prosperity resulting from foresight.
Fives	Changes, adjustments, restlessness. Flighty and fighty. Seeking excitement, no matter the consequences. Five pips show something/someone upsetting the status quo.
Five of Hearts	A surprise about a lover or loved one. Emotional disturbances. Jealousy in love.
Five of Diamonds	Troubles or conflicts because of different ideas or opinions. Tempers, your own and other people's.

Card	Meanings
Five of Clubs	Disharmony and quarrels. Division, upsets, and unexpected obstacles.
Five of Spades	Quarrels and disputes. Turmoil and disorder. Plans going wrong. Separation and tears.
Sixes	Balance, diplomacy, harmony. A steady path. Protection and comfort. Six pips show a straight and easy road ahead.
Six of Hearts	Children and their world. Established affection, love, and pleasant invitations.
Six of Diamonds	Contentment and happiness. Visitors, good tidings, and pleasant events.
Six of Clubs	Happy and fortunate meetings. A run of good luck. Opportunities appear.
Six of Spades	Unexpected failure of a plan. Discouragement. Keep a cool head.
Sevens	Uniqueness, introspection, unusual events. Fated and destined events that shake one up, for better or for worse. Seven pips show a pivot from the path.
Seven of Hearts	Arguments between lovers. Sexual encounters and affairs. Favours that may not be all that they seem.
Seven of Diamonds	Financial losses, recklessness, risk-taking. Unfriendly criticism or gossip.
Seven of Clubs	Worries over money, financial losses. Wasted time, impatience with delays.
Seven of Spades	Quarrels with partners. Break-ups. Accidents and misunderstandings. Hold off on making big decisions.
Eights	Solid, steady progress. An abundance of growth which may be too much. Eight pips show an upcoming harvest.
Eight of Hearts	Gifts given and received with love. Happy spending. Love that grows.
Eight of Diamonds	Exciting news, messages from afar. Holidays and journeys. Change. Study and academic work or physical education.
Eight of Clubs	Money or assets acquired through careful planning or investment. Important documents or letters relating to business or money matters.
Eight of Spades	Relief that something has ended. Unexpected arrivals and departures. Surprising events.

Card	Meanings
Nines	Change, exploration, new experiences. Giving for giving's sake, the gift of charity, both giving and receiving. Nine pips show a centred approach brings the greatest rewards.
Nine of Hearts	The wish card. Desires fulfilled. Success and abundance.
Nine of Diamonds	Prosperity, change for the better, productive disagreements.
Nine of Clubs	Contentment and achievement. Appreciation of life. A gathering of friends brings fulfillment.
Nine of Spades	Quarrels, rejection. Change is required. Events that are unwanted but necessary.
Tens	Completion, endings, manifestations. The end brings new beginnings. Accomplishment and success. Ten pips mirror each other to show reflection.
Ten of Hearts	Great happiness and good fortune. Unexpected good news.
Ten of Diamonds	Finances. Legal matters. Fast decisions. Journeys to somewhere new.
Ten of Clubs	New beginnings. An important journey. Rewards for hard work.
Ten of Spades	Disappointment, tears, grief. The end of the road, a new path must be found.
Jacks	Youthful joy and arrogance. Messages of/about other people. Self-belief and self-absorption. The mutable signs of the zodiac.
Jack of Hearts	A young or youthful person with pleasure on their mind. Easy on the eyes and heart, love and good times are favoured over the mundane.
Jack of Diamonds	A young or youthful person with a busy mind full of mischief and worries. Impulsive and brave, patience is not a strong suit. Money comes and goes fast.
Jack of Clubs	A young or youthful person, thoughtful and helpful. Athletic and energetic, things seem to fall into place.
Jack of Spades	A young or youthful person with an agreeable personality. Quick-witted and interesting. Manners are not a strong point, nor are the practicalities of life.

Card	Meanings
Queens	Feminine energies and symbolism. Nurturing, caring, intuition. Message of/about feminine people. The fixed signs of the zodiac.
Queen of Hearts	A mature, feminine person with a generous and loving heart. Creative and expressive emotionally. Loyal and empathetic. Social and charming.
Queen of Diamonds	A mature, feminine person with a strong, forceful personality. Fast thinking and assertive. Can be cutting with words if angry or offended.
Queen of Clubs	A mature, feminine person, adaptable and affectionate. Dramatic and lively. A savvy business mind and responsible investments create financial comfort.
Queen of Spades	A mature, feminine person who tries to keep their emotions restrained. Strong-willed and rational. A faithful friend once you have earned their respect. Noted for their polite charm, liveliness, and sociability.
Kings	Masculine energies and symbolism. Authority, status, leadership. Messages of/about masculine people. The cardinal signs of the zodiac.
King of Hearts	A mature, masculine, authoritative person with a wealth of experience readily shared. Charismatic, fair-minded, generous. Wears their heart on their sleeve though they try to hide it. Good humoured and tender-hearted.
King of Diamonds	A mature, masculine, authoritative person, sharp and perceptive. Confident, edgy, inclined to vanity. A go-getter who makes their own luck and never passes up an opportunity. Sarcastic and witty.
King of Clubs	A mature, masculine, authoritative person, energetic and lively. Wise and practical. Hard to get to know, but loyal and steady once trust is earned.
King of Spades	A mature, masculine, authoritative person, strong-willed and rational. Emotions are kept hidden and rules are important. Sees things as only black or white but holds high principles and expects all to live up to them.
The Jokers	The Jokers represent the unknown or the unexpected. When a Joker appears in a reading a new path previously not considered appears. Whether this is a viable route to take depends on the surrounding cards. As a person, the Jokers indicate outliers and eccentrics who make and follow their own rules.

About Sandra Lee

Sandra Lee has been avidly divining the future in one way or another since she learned to pull petals off daisies while chanting about love as a child. While she no longer desecrates flowers without permission from the plant before she harvests them, she still chants, albeit off-key, about the mysteries of love and the world around her.

Ritual and divination have been a huge part of Sandra's life since before she even knew what it was that she was doing and remains the foundation on which she structures her life. Born with a deep love and respect for nature, Sandra has been an enthusiastic practitioner of all things magickal and esoteric her whole adult life.

Over the decades Sandra has investigated and utilised many forms of divination to try and make sense of the world and people around her and cartomancy remains a comforting daily practice. With a passion for knowledge and a need to know the 'why' of everything, divination has guided Sandra through many adventures and travails so far in this lifetime.

Learning the art of cartomancy subliminally through her childhood, and literally ever since, led to dabbling in a variety of wonderful and wily forms of witchery and esoterica. As a professional astrologer specialising in magical elections, Sandra loves nothing more than slipping into something spiritual and getting busy creating beautiful potions and talismans when the stars and planets align.

Fancying herself a dab hand in the kitchen, a lover of both chaos and order, a green thumb in the garden, and a scriber of beautiful sigils, Sandra's beloveds would be inclined to add that she is also a hoarder of books and music, with an uncanny ability to locate truly wyrd and unique items within minutes of walking into an op shop.

After working with her goddesses at dawn each day to give thanks and celebrate the new day, Sandra steps into the real world to work with information and knowledge resources as a library technician. She spends her time off moving furniture around in her home to fit in even more books, music, and op shop finds. You can contact Sandra at stellarleeastrology@gmail.com

Tarot and Divination

By Linda Marson

How does Tarot work? Why does a 'good' Tarot reading leave you wondering how cards you selected provide advice that makes sense to you?

I've been using Tarot as a divination tool since the late 1980s. For me, the answer is 'magic' mixed with some old-fashioned structured learning using the Waite-Smith deck first published in 1909. Symbols and imagery in the 22 Major Arcana cards are based on European decks known collectively as Marseille style decks. However, academic and mystic, Arthur Edward Waite, a member of the Hermetic Order of the Golden Dawn, changed some of the original imagery to incorporate Kabbalistic and other occult practices.

Artist, theatre designer and storyteller, Pamela Colman-Smith, was given free rein to illustrate the 56 cards of the Minor Arcana. She revolutionised the look of the 40 number cards of the four suits by incorporating basic numerological concepts into illustrations based on an understanding of the four elements of Water (Cups), Air (Swords), Fire (Wands) and Earth (Pentacles). The Waite-Smith deck quickly became a worldwide best seller and the model for other decks, including the *DruidCraft Tarot* where Druid and Wicca concepts are built into the Minor Arcana stories.

Run forward to 1980 when Rachel Pollack first published her groundbreaking book, *78 Degrees of Wisdom*. Here she drew a parallel between The Fool's journey and Joseph Campbell's concept of the hero's journey as described in his book *The Hero with a Thousand Faces* published in 1949. The result is a divinatory tool that provides insight into where you are on the archetypal adventure. Are you simply dealing with things in the ordinary, everyday world or have you crossed a threshold into a special world where you are fighting 'demons'? Or have you dealt with the demons and find yourself returning to the ordinary world with insight and wisdom?

Even if you don't like the old-fashioned images in the Waite-Smith deck, I encourage you to play a while with these cards. You may well find you develop a deeper understanding of, or different perspective on the Tarot deck you usually use.

The Major Arcana

Let's dive straight into Rachel Pollack's analysis of the 22 Major Arcana cards which are numbered zero (The Fool) to 21 (The World). These cards represent the major secrets or archetypal behaviour patterns that motivate people. They illustrate stages in the personal journeys we make in all aspects of our lives – from relationships to career to leisure pursuits. Symbolically, we start all journeys as The Fool, the Tarot card that represents new beginnings, where we leave the baggage of the past behind, start out afresh and trust that the Universe will provide. As the journey proceeds, we use the tools at our disposal (The Magician), listen to our intuition (The High Priestess), let opportunities grow and blossom (The Empress), face challenges, take time out for reflection, overcome personal doubts and inhibitions, make changes, discard what we do not need, and achieve our goals in the final card of The World.

Rachel Pollack shows how the Major Arcana falls naturally into three rows of seven cards, with The Fool (numbered zero) sitting outside. In its stand-alone position, The Fool represents the soul incarnating into a body, the moment you decide to step into the archetypal patterns represented by the other 21 cards. The three rows reflect Joseph Campbell's concept of three stages in what he calls 'the hero's journey'. The first row (The Magician to The Chariot) represents the outer concerns of life in society. The second row (Strength to Temperance) is the subconscious which we enter when presented with a challenge in the outer world (Campbell calls this 'the call to adventure'). Who am I? What patterns of behaviour drive me? Do I need to release some of them to pursue my true purpose in life? These are the questions you ask yourself as you move towards the equilibrium of Temperance.

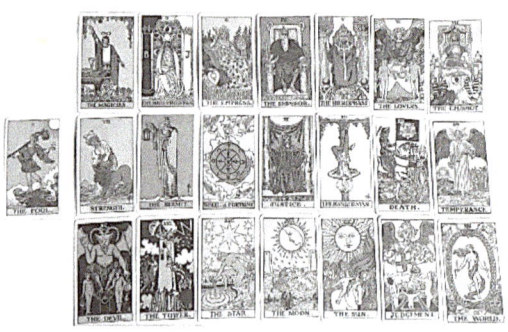

After rising to the challenge, we journey back to our everyday life – The Devil to The World. You have glimpsed your true purpose in life, but now you must develop spiritually and understand how you interact with the forces of the Universe. This is the realm of the superconscious, where you connect with universal energies. You go on a journey from dark to light – from the black cards of The Devil and The Tower, through three forms of light (The Star, The Moon, and The Sun) and emerge to rejoice in your transformation (Judgement). You are at one with the Universe, in the place you're meant to be (The World).

It's an exhilarating journey that we all take in different areas of our lives all the time. We experience the energy of the Major Arcana cards at both a macro and a micro level. When you decide to marry, have children, move house, start a new job, leave an old job, leave a relationship, get a divorce – these are macro-level experiences or major turning points in your life. Leaving a job could be represented by the Death card, deciding to marry by The Lovers. However, the same cards could refer to micro-level experiences, for example, having to choose between two holiday destinations could be represented by The Lovers. The cards cannot be read in isolation – you should always look at other cards in the spread to see the full story.

The Fool is all about taking a leap of faith – similar, in many ways, to The Joker in a traditional deck of playing cards. If you get stuck in the energy of The Hanged Man, for example, invoke the energy of The Fool, take a leap of faith and trust that if you let go of what you're 'hanging onto' something better will emerge and allow you to move toward accepting the change signalled in the next card, Death.

To help you understand the key themes of each Major Arcana card, here are questions to ask yourself when they appear in a reading.

The Fool
1. Am I ready to make a completely new start in some area of my life?
2. Have I said goodbye to things in my past that are of no use to me in the future?
3. Am I taking useful lessons from the past into the future?
4. Do I have faith in my ability to make the right decisions and act accordingly?
5. Do I have faith in my ability to overcome any hurdles I might encounter on this new journey?

The Magician
1. Am I ready to use all the skills at my disposal to achieve my goal?
2. Am I aware of the power I have to make things happen?
3. Am I in tune with the energies of the Universe around me?
4. Can I channel those energies into something real and tangible?
5. Am I clear about my intentions and motivations?

The High Priestess
1. What is my inner voice, my intuition, telling me to do?
2. Do I need to withdraw from everyday life so that I can tune into my inner voice?
3. Is there a woman I can talk to about this issue – a woman whose wisdom and opinions I respect?
4. Do I have the courage to act on my intuition?
5. Do I have the self-awareness to distinguish between intuition and illusions based on false hopes and desires?

The Empress
1. Do I understand that only by accepting others for who they are, can I truly express love?
2. Do I understand how powerful and important self-love is?
3. Do I allow myself the freedom to relax and grow?
4. Am I willing to let those I love be independent and live their own lives?
5. Am I free of the urge to smother or restrict the growth of people or projects that I love?
6. Are there creative paths or endeavours I would like to nurture and develop?

The Emperor
1. Do I have the self-discipline to see projects through to their conclusion?
2. Am I in a position to set directions and oversee the growth of an enterprise?
3. Am I prepared to be systematic in my approach to things?
4. Am I ready to take a leadership role?
5. Am I acting fairly and justly in a leadership role?
6. Do I have a role in establishing law and order?

7. Do I have the courage to move out of the comfort zone created by the successful position I'm in and accept new challenges?

The Hierophant
1. Is there an institution whose values I accept without question?
2. Is conforming to the prevailing views in society a major motivating force in my life?
3. Am I prepared to question the values and belief system I grew up with?
4. Do I act according to the views or doctrines of another person in my life?
5. Am I prepared to take responsibility for my own spiritual development?
6. Should I find a mentor or undertake study to help me develop on a spiritual level?
7. Am I in a position to help others develop their spirituality?

The Lovers
1. Can I make decisions that I am prepared to live with for the rest of my life?
2. Can I live honestly with the decisions I make?
3. Can I resist temptations that could lead me to act without integrity?
4. Am I prepared to make ethical and moral choices, to choose between right and wrong?
5. Do I know where I stand on issues? Can I make up my own mind, without relying on the views of others?
6. Am I about to fall in love, to enter the first romantic phase of a relationship?
7. Am I ready to move into a new, deeper phase of a relationship?

The Chariot
1. Am I ready to claim victory?
2. Do I have the determination and willpower to control opposing forces in my life?
3. Can I control my emotions without denying their existence?
4. Can I concentrate all my energies on achieving my goals?
5. Do I have the confidence to carve out a role and identity for myself?
6. Am I ready to take control of my own destiny?

Strength
1. Do I have the confidence to believe in my own reserves of inner strength?
2. Am I prepared to show compassion for others as I find a path through difficult situations?
3. Am I prepared to relax and trust that difficult situations can be resolved without exerting undue pressure on others?
4. Do I have the courage to acknowledge my inner fears and desires, and triumph despite them?
5. Am I prepared to be patient and persevere to find the right path through a situation?
6. Do I trust myself enough to reveal my hidden passions and emotions, confident in the knowledge that they won't get out of control?

The Hermit
1. Do I have the courage to be alone with my thoughts?
2. Am I afraid of being alone?
3. Am I ready to search within for the next step on my path to personal and spiritual fulfilment?
4. Am I willing to take a risk, to leave the safe world behind and do what I truly want to do?
5. Is there a wise person in my life who could help me find my true path?
6. Do I have the wisdom to provide spiritual guidance to others?

The Wheel of Fortune
1. Am I prepared to go with the changes that are around me now?
2. Do I see that I have reached a turning point in some aspect of my life?
3. Do I grab opportunities and use them to my advantage?
4. Am I aware of the patterns that shape my life and my behaviour?
5. Am I prepared to change those patterns if they only ever pull me down?
6. Do I go with the flow of things, accepting that every situation has its highs and lows?

Justice
1. Do I accept that my past actions have shaped where I am today?
2. Am I prepared to accept the consequences of what I do?

3. Am I prepared to take responsibility for my own actions?
4. Do I consider all sides of an issue and make fair decisions based on that analysis?
5. Do I always respect justice, and act fairly and ethically?
6. Am I dealing with a legal situation that has implications for my future? If so, am I prepared to negotiate a fair solution?

The Hanged Man
1. Do I have outmoded attitudes and behaviour patterns that are holding me back? If so, am I prepared to surrender them in the knowledge that, by doing so, I can move forward and take control of my life?
2. Do I have the courage to move outside my comfort zone and view things from a different perspective?
3. Do I have the patience to wait for things to follow their natural course of development?
4. Do I have the strength and self-awareness to accept situations for what they really are, and people for who they really are?

Death
1. Am I ready to make a major change in some aspect of my life?
2. Do I accept that making major changes in my life can mean leaving people and situations behind?
3. Have I released feelings of resentment, anger or frustration associated with people or situations that I am leaving behind?
4. Can I close the door on old patterns of behaviour, comfortable with the notion that what replaces them will be better?
5. Am I ready to move forward into the bright new phase that awaits me?

Temperance
1. Have I reached a point where everything is in balance, where I have found the right blend of ingredients?
2. Do I know the value of my ability to bring opposites together, to create harmony and a sense of peace around me?
3. Am I enjoying a period of health and wellbeing?
4. Do I have a sense of where my life is heading, of my true purpose in life?

5. Am I secure in the knowledge that I am ready to journey forth and achieve my life's purpose?
6. Am I making plans to travel?

The Devil
1. Do I feel chained to a situation or person because of deep-seated fears which I cannot even name?
2. Is my behaviour in relation to a situation or relationship obsessive and self-destructive?
3. Do I feel powerless to change situations I find myself in, thereby denying responsibility for my own actions or behaviour?
4. Do I manipulate people or situations so that I can blame others for my woes?
5. Do I have the courage to look honestly at myself and acknowledge that I have the power to remove the chains that bind me?

The Tower
1. Am I ready to flow with changes that are being forced upon me by unexpected events?
2. Can I accept that these changes are necessary?
3. Do I know what I need to release from the past to get through this turbulent time?
4. Do I see that my own reluctance to change could have precipitated the current dramatic events?
5. Do I have the self-awareness to look beyond the immediate turmoil and see that something positive is likely to emerge?
6. Do I have the flexibility to rebuild a situation or relationship which has suffered because of sudden and unexpected events?

The Star
1. Am I ready to relax and trust that the worst is behind me?
2. Am I experiencing a time of healing where I can focus once more on my true purpose in life?
3. What area of my life needs renewing?
4. Is it time for me to express creatively the inspiration and wisdom I receive from the Universe?
5. How best can I use my wisdom to inspire others?
6. Do I appreciate how blessed I am?

The Moon
1. Am I having disturbing dreams which seem to carry messages from my subconscious?
2. Do I realise that my dreams are triggers that will help me understand my motives and emotional conditioning?
3. Are issues with my mother or the nature of motherhood coming to the surface?
4. Am I coming to terms with hidden, secret things that have long dwelt in the realm of the subconscious?
5. Am I feeling depressed or moody for no apparent reason?
6. Can I use the messages coming from my subconscious to inspire creative works?

The Sun
1. Do I know how to be happy and to express my inner child?
2. Do I fully appreciate the wonderful opportunities open to me now to make a new start in life?
3. How can I express my creativity?
4. Do I appreciate how well I've dealt with difficult situations?

Judgement
1. Am I rejoicing at major transformations I have made in my life?
2. Am I ready to move on and wholeheartedly embrace the next phase of my life?
3. Am I prepared to take responsibility for everything I have done so far?
4. Am I ready to answer the call, to do what I feel drawn to?
5. Do I appreciate how liberating it will be to answer the call, to be reborn?
6. Is an event in my life 20 years ago, relevant to something that's happening now?

The World
1. Am I currently feeling a sense of achievement at reaching a goal?
2. Am I savouring the feeling that I'm in a place where the world wants me to be?
3. Are my successes being acknowledged by others?
4. Could my current achievements lead to other successful ventures?

5. Have I used my talents to create something which helps others understand the ways of the Universe?

The Minor Arcana

The 56 cards of the Minor Arcana depict the activities, emotions, and personalities we encounter every day and provide the context for the Major Arcana cards in a reading. There are 40 numbered cards – from Ace to Ten across four suits which relate to the four elements.

Suit	Element	Emotions / personalities	Activities
Wands	Fire	Energy, passion, spirit, action.	What we **create**.
Swords	Air	Intellect, communication, past hurt/pain.	What we **think**.
Cups	Water	Emotions, feelings, psychic energy.	What we **feel**.
Pentacles	Earth	Manifestation, material world.	What we **do** and how we do it.

  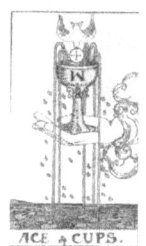 

Key themes for each number:

Number	Key themes
Ace I	Beginning, gift, initiation, new opportunity.
Two II	Duality, choice, balance, partnership.
Three III	Creativity, growth, collaboration.
Four IV	Stability, foundation, structure/boundaries.
Five V	Change, conflict, mundane troubles, lack of communication.
Six VI	Balance, give and take, integration, peace, love, healing.

Number	Key themes
Seven VII	Unexpected change, insight, seeker, don't give up.
Eight VIII	Success, abundance, strength, personal power.
Nine IX	Wisdom/insight, selfless giving, culmination/completion, 'on cloud 9'.
Ten X	Ending, legacy, final message, result.

Court cards are the people or personality cards of the Minor Arcana. My first way of reading court cards is to relate them to the person I'm doing the reading for. I see them as personality traits or ways people are behaving or responding to issues around the questions they ask.

In this sense, they are gender-neutral and should be read as indicating levels of maturity. Pages are the least mature, then the Knights, followed by the Queens and Kings as the most mature. Keep in mind that a 60-year-old person could manifest as a Page of Swords if, for example, their spouse had recently died and they were now responsible for managing the finances of the family business, a task they had never done before. The Page of Swords would indicate a lack of confidence in their ability to do this.

Court cards can, of course, refer to other people, particularly in a position such as the external environment in relation to an issue. Also, if the reading is about family, friends or work colleagues, court cards are likely to represent one or more people involved in the situation.

Get the question right!

The key to divining with Tarot is to ask a clear question. Avoid closed questions which invite only a 'yes' or 'no' answer. Ask open questions like 'what's the best way for me to deal with the problems I'm having at work / in my relationship / with my health?' (and so on). When people come to me for a reading, I start by explaining that, for me, seeking answers to questions using the Tarot is all about tuning into your Higher Self. "The magic of the Tarot", I say, "is that the cards you select while thinking of your question or even repeating it out loud, channel messages from your own inner wisdom, stuff you already know. This is *your* story. As a Tarot reader, I'm here to help you read that story."

Specifying a timeframe for your questions is important and don't go years into the future. Factors beyond your control can affect a situation if you try to look too far into the future. Also, the questions should be about what *you*

can do or learn. Don't ask questions about what other people might do in a situation. Typical questions I help clients formulate include:
- What do I need to know about my relationship/ my work situation/ my spiritual path over the next six months?
- What's the best way for me to approach the job interview next week?
- What's the best way for me to deal with the conflict at work / in my marriage/ with my daughter?

For questions like these, I use this layout (below) where each position has a meaning attached to it. After discussing the message coming from the cards about the question asked, I usually ask clients to select three cards to provide more information about the 'answer' card in position four.

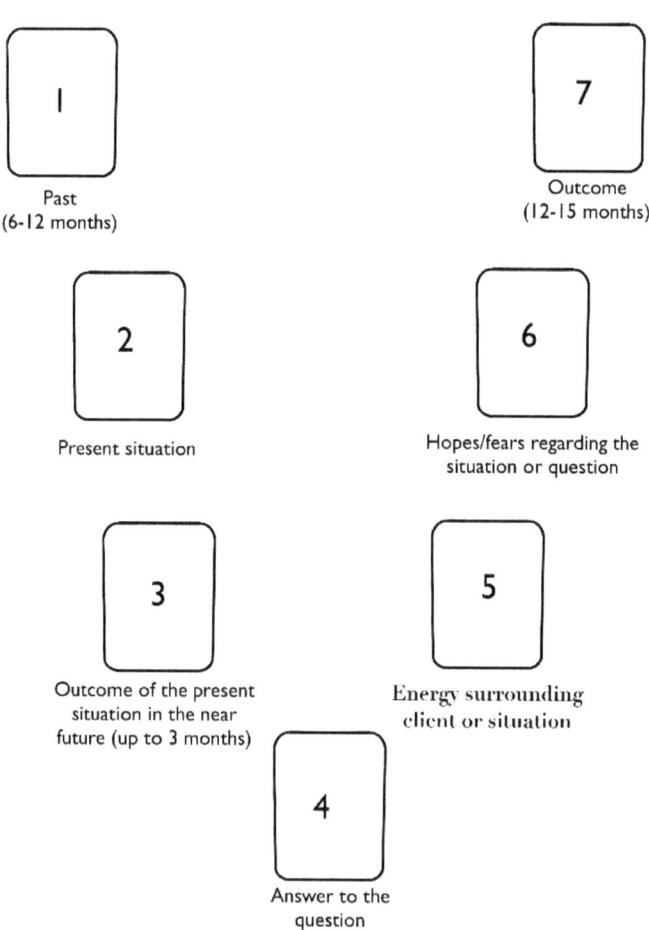

Read the pictures!

Now comes the fun part – doing a layout and interpreting the cards. This is where the Waite-Smith deck with a storyline to the 40 numbered cards of the Minor Arcana really comes into its own. I often start my day by asking these three questions:

1. What do I need to focus on today? (4 Swords)
2. In relation to that, what should I NOT do? (3 Pentacles)
3. In relation to that, what should I DO (9 Swords)

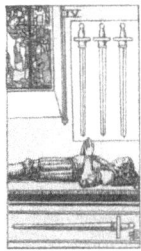

Here's how I would approach the interpretation. All cards come from the Minor Arcana, so no major archetypal energies are operating.

- *Card 1* – Take a rest from too much thinking and mental activity. The image tells the story – the person is lying down, has put three swords up on the wall and the other one is nearby ready to be picked up when the time is right.
- *Card 2* – *Don't* continue working on the practical aspects of building something. The image has two people discussing plans with a craftsperson/builder.
- *Card 3* – The 9 of Swords is one of the most common cards to appear in a reading. Why? Because people tend to want a Tarot reading when they are worried about something. For me, the key to its interpretation lies in two visual aspects of the image. The quilt on the bed is bright and colourful, decorated with the signs of the zodiac. There may be nine swords on the wall, but you can't see their points. What's the

message? Have the courage to open your eyes and you'll see that the Universe is open to you and that what you've been worrying about is pointless!

Let's move to the same three-card layout, but with a more open timeframe.
1. What do I need to focus on in terms of my relationship with person X? (4 Cups)
2. In relation to that, what should I NOT do? (7 Cups)
3. In relation to that, what should I DO? (Strength)

Here's how I would approach the interpretation...

The question is about a relationship, so two cards from the suit of Cups make sense and indicate that feelings are involved. The Major Arcana card, the first in the second line of the hero/heroine's journey, suggests that the person may be about to enter a challenging time in the relationship.

- *Card 1* - Don't keep focussing on what you already know about the relationship (the three cups on the ground). Have the courage to open your arms, look up and see that the Universe is offering you something more in this relationship. Note how this message comes from looking at the picture and bringing it to life.
- *Card 2* - You can see the contents of six cups, that is, you already know much about the relationship. However, at the moment, it's not helpful to focus on what you can't see (the contents of the top cup). In other words, stop daydreaming, stop trying to see what's in the seventh cup.

✦ *Card 3* - Know that you have the inner strength to handle anything the Universe throws at you in terms of this relationship. Here I suggest you look at the list of questions to ask if Strength appears in a reading. Since this is about a relationship, it could be indicating that the person needs to trust themselves to reveal hidden passions and emotions, confident in the knowledge they can remain in control.

Conclusion

I hope my practical approach to reading the cards has been helpful. There are many more tips in the satchel, which, like The Fool, I carry over my shoulder as I journey through life. If you would like to know more about the classes and products I offer, check out the information in my biography.

About Linda Marson

Linda has been reading and teaching Tarot for more years than she cares to remember! She's a former President of the Tarot Guild of Australia *and founder of* Global Spiritual Studies. *In 2017, she created* TarotNav – a GPS for Life, *a unique guide to reading Tarot for yourself. This multimedia product contains short videos illustrating the meaning of all Major Arcana cards, an eBook with simple meanings for all 78 cards, layouts for doing readings and a workbook to keep track of your readings.*

See globalspiritualstudies.com/linda-marson-tarot-teacher *for information on* TarotNav, *Linda's* Live and Learn the Tarot *course and other classes she offers through* Global Spiritual Studies.

Since 2013, Linda has been helping with the organisation of Gothic Image Tours (gothicimagetours.co.uk) *to sacred and spiritual sites in the UK and Ireland. During tours, Linda facilitates a process for using Tarot to explore the messages these ancient sites and landscapes have for each person.*

Oracle Cards

By Sandra Greenhalgh

Some information in this chapter is also relevant for Tarot cards.

Oracle cards include images, symbols, and/or words which open the querent to the wisdom of the archetypal world. Unlike Tarot cards, there are no established rules about the number of cards in an oracle deck or their design. Some oracle cards have individualised backs, some include images without text, and others have text without images. Decks of oracle cards can be delightfully different, which can make choosing the 'right' deck for yourself quite difficult.

Speaking of difficult, don't fall into the trap of thinking that because they are 'just' oracle cards, they are easy to use or simple to interpret. Some oracle decks are extraordinarily dense with layers of meanings and background information. On the other hand, many oracle decks can be used straight away without needing to first learn and memorise a complex system.

Another advantage to oracle cards is that they are often ideal to use when you want to draw just one single card for inspiration and guidance. That's a major plus for the busy witch or seer!

How to choose a deck

You walk into a store selling oracle cards. Around you are shelves and shelves packed full of glorious oracle decks, of different sizes, colours, prices, and designs. How do you choose the one that is best for you? Here's some hints to help you:

- The image on the case/pack calls to you. You can't stop looking at it or holding in your hand.
- The deck has been recommended by someone you respect.
- You love the size of the deck and the glide of the cards.

- ✦ You've done your due diligence by researching online. If you like cats, do an internet search for 'cat oracles'. There is a wealth of information (and images) available online for most decks, though don't be immediately turned off a deck if you read one bad review. In every domain, there are people not satisfied with a product, or have an issue (real or imagined) with the creator/s.
- ✦ Check out Tarot or oracle groups, posts on social media, or online videos.
- ✦ A favourite author or illustrator has published a deck, and you love their work. Bonus points if they are an Australian creator!

It's OK to have more than one deck of oracle cards, as some decks seem to align better with certain situations or queries.

A fantastic way to find a new (and unique) deck is by searching an online crowdfunding platform such as Kickstarter or Indigogo. There are of course potential (though rare) pitfalls associated with backing the creation of a deck via this method, particularly as deadlines can be exceeded by months, or years. It's certainly not a good option if you want immediate gratification and the feel of your new deck in your hands as soon as possible.

If you receive a deck as a gift, that makes deciding easy, as it's been done for you. But don't be afraid to re-gift or sell a deck if you don't like it or can't connect with it despite numerous attempts. Some relationships just aren't meant to be. On the other hand, it's easy to quickly accumulate a collection of oracle decks, which soon becomes a hoard, overflowing from shelves and boxes. Don't say I didn't warn you.

Counterfeit decks

Unfortunately, counterfeit desks – both Tarot and oracle – are widely available, particularly through online retailers who offer extremely low prices. An unusually low price point is the best sign that the deck might be counterfeit. Often counterfeit decks are poor quality and flimsy, or smaller in size than the original, and it's not worth paying the cheaper price. They may also not 'feel' right; after all, they began with the theft of someone's creative work. Buying (and selling) a counterfeit deck is commercially and professionally harmful to the creator of the original deck.

If you do decide to buy decks online, please make your purchase through a reputable marketplace. There are also excellent second-hand buy and sell groups on social media sites that cater specifically for Australians.

Usually, having a QR code on the box rather than an enclosed booklet is a giveaway sign you are about to purchase a counterfeit deck. Sadly, that's not an absolute indication, as some independent ('indie') creators keep prices down by offering an electronic guide rather than a physical booklet.

The best way to avoid buying ripped-off or counterfeit decks is to purchase them directly from the creator, if they have a website. Speaking from personal experience as an indie creator, I love selling directly to people. It brings me much joy to pop a carefully wrapped deck into a mailing bag. Alternatively, for mass market decks, buy from an Australian indie retailer – most of them would never sell counterfeit decks, as that's against their ethos and they are aware that they would lose customers and credibility by doing so.

How to read with oracle cards

There is no one set methodology to dictate how you should use your oracle deck. Often the accompanying guidebook will give you some ideas, but you don't have to stick to those options. My preferred methods of working with oracle cards are:

- ✦ Decide whether to read reversed (upside down) cards, and check the accompanying guidebook to see if there are reversed meanings provided. If you'd prefer to read the cards upright (right way up), quickly check through the deck before shuffling.

- ✦ Consider the purpose of your reading. Do you have a specific question or just want some general guidance? Try to avoid asking questions which only have a yes or no answer unless your deck is designed for this purpose.

- ✦ Decide how many cards you are going to draw. If you are drawing more than two, perhaps you would like to place them into a spread or pattern. A three-card spread is an easy option. Place one card to signify past influences, one card for present circumstances, and the final card for potential future outcomes.

- ✦ As you shuffle the cards, think about your question, and aim of the reading.

- ✦ When it feels right, choose the card/s to gain insight or spark your intuition. Different ways to do this include taking a card from the top or bottom of the deck or fanning out the deck then intuitively choosing one from the middle or, alternatively, use a card that falls from the deck while shuffling.

✦ After you have chosen the card/s, place it in front of you. Empty your mind. Focus on the images or words on the oracle card. What 'jumps out' at you? Is it a particular colour? Or part of an image such as a person's face? Or perhaps you have a certain feeling or emotion as you gaze upon a card, which may or may not link with the actual imagery? Take notice of these flashes of insight. I've provided a practical example of how to do this in the next section. If possible, journal your experiences for ongoing reflections.

✦ Do some further research about the card/s by reading the guidebook for additional information.

✦ If you like, take a photo of the card on your phone so you can refer to it during the day, or leave the card on your altar or in a prominent position.

Example of an intuitive reading

Sometimes, I like to receive succinct advice without referring to the guidebook. Here's an example of how I would intuitively read messages from a single card, using the *Druid Wisdom Oracle* deck.

My focus is to receive advice about travel plans. I first meditate and shuffle the deck, paying attention to my travel-focused query. I've decided to draw just the one card located at the top of the deck.

This turns out to be the Epona card. The image includes a green cloaked woman riding side saddle on a white horse. She holds roses in a bowl which has an image of crossed keys. Under the card name there are three words – *sovereignty, journeys, protection*.

I quieten my mind, and the first thing that strikes me is the lively pace of the white horse, stepping boldly along the path. It creates a sense of movement, of going forward. The woman has a smile upon her face, which inspires a feeling of pleasure and happy anticipation. I feel a sense of serenity looking at the green hues and the peaceful blue sky behind horse and rider. Finally, my eyes are drawn to the words *journeys* and *protection*.

My take-away message from the Epona card is that I should progress with making my travel plans, as it's likely that I will have a fantastic time. The way is open, and I'm unlikely to meet with any overwhelming restrictions. All that information was intuitively received, and I didn't need to refer to the guidebook.

How to store your oracle cards

Generally, oracle cards are larger in size than Tarot cards, though some decks are available in 'pocket' size, which are handy to pop into your bag or pocket. Many people prefer to keep their oracle decks stored in the original box or container, as often the container is a feature of the deck. While some Tarot decks are sold with flimsy cardboard 'tuckboxes', generally oracle cards are sold in a sturdy box, bag or case which is easy to open and store. Alternatively, if you'd like to keep your cards in a separate box or cloth, that is completely your call. Do whatever works best for you.

What to do when you receive a new deck

Personally, I like to get to know my oracle or Tarot deck slowly. At times, I don't take a new deck out of the shrink wrap for months, until I have the time and headspace to engage with it properly.

You may feel the urge to cleanse and bless your deck before using it. In this case, I do not recommend using a spritz or water-based method if your cards are made of paper. Instead, try leaving the cards with a suitable crystal, or on the windowsill in the moonlight, or smoke cleanse with incense or dropped leaves from local native flora such as Eucalyptus trees. Keeping your new deck beside your bed or under your pillow is a nice way of becoming attuned with it.

Until I'm familiar with a new deck and feel comfortable with it, I'll keep the cards in their original order, which makes it easier to cross reference with the booklet or guide. I will gently lay the cards, one by one, on a clean surface and glance at each image. As I am by nature an impatient person, this usually occurs quite quickly. If a particular card 'jumps out at me', I will place it separately as a prompt to read the guidebook and learn more about the background information. Then, finally, I'll shuffle the cards and do a simple reading and verify the results for accuracy.

Some readers like to do a 'deck interview' as a method for learning about the characteristics of the deck. This process includes asking questions such as what are the strengths, limits or weaknesses, and unique personality of the deck, then drawing a corresponding card to answer these questions.

> A deck that 'sings' to you is easy to work with upfront. Other decks take more time to warm to, but can be well worth the effort.

Trimming and edging

Some people like to trim the edges of their cards, to remove the borders around the images. This also reduces the size of large cards for people with small hands. While some cards have beautifully coloured or gilt edges, many have plain edges, so creating personalised edge artwork (or colours) is also something people like to do. Check online for tutorials about how to do this, bearing in mind that if you are planning on reselling your cards in the future, alterations will reduce the market price of your deck.

Disposing of a damaged or incomplete deck

Thankfully, I've never had to dispose of an old, much-loved deck. My original Tarot deck is over 35 years and is still going strong – probably because I am diligent with hand washing, and shuffle gently. However, if your deck is no longer able to be used because of damage, or lost cards, ask the deck how it wishes to be transformed. Here are some options:

- Offer the existing cards to other people. You'd be surprised how people can 'rebirth' cards into decoupage or crafty creations, or perhaps they are missing some cards from their own deck and would appreciate the additions.
- Ask in an online forum if other people have your missing cards and would they be willing to send them to you. Yes, this does happen!
- Create personalised greeting cards by cutting and pasting the images onto cardboard.
- Use the cards in spell work.
- If appropriate, reverently bury or burn the cards, after saying your farewells.

Here's a lovely idea if you are replacing an old/worn out deck with a new deck. Take each of the new cards, and intersperse them behind their counterpart in the old deck. Then carefully wrap up the two combined decks in a cloth of natural fibres for a defined interval of time (for example, a lunar cycle or a day and a night). The concept behind this idea is that the old, experienced deck magically imparts its wisdom and energy into the new deck. Here are some words you might like to say to help strengthen the magical connections:

From old to new,
Essence through and through.
Ancient wisdom is shared,
As these cards are paired.

About Sandra Greenhalgh

Sandra is an author, artist and occultist who lives in Brisbane, Australia. A long-term participant, student, and teacher of Western Mystery traditions, she joined The Order of Bards, Ovates and Druids in 1988, while working in England.

Growing up in the Queensland countryside helped foster her deep love of the wild places of bush, beach, and the outback. Whenever possible, Sandra retreats to camping beside the ocean with her extended family and friends.

Sandra has over 30 years of Neopagan community involvement. Tarot and divination are passions, and in 2019 Sandra created a new deck of oracle cards focussing on Druidic lore, called the Druid Wisdom Oracle. *She also authored the* Druid Wisdom Oracle Guidebook, *released in 2020.*

In 2020, Sandra co-edited and contributed to A History of Druidry in Australia, *which includes contributions from over thirty Australians who practise Druidry. She is author and co-editor of* Living Witchery: Beginner Witch Guide *(released 2021).*

Sandra is grateful to live with her husband, two grown children and a couple of spoilt cats. Between writing, drawing, and procrastinating, she works in healthcare.

See byrningtyger.com *for more information.*

FLOURISH: Next Steps

Are you ready to bump up your practices? Maybe you'd like to head down the business side of things and get paid for your readings?

This section – by Alexandra, Kim, and Sandra - will help show you the way!

Reading For Other People

Many of us feel the pull to test our psychic skills with a querent at some stage. Divining for other people offers both challenges and opportunities, and we will walk you through these in this chapter. While some information applies to professional (paid) sessions, most of the advice is useful even when doing a freebie reading for your Aunty Mabel.

Reading for a close friend or sympathetic family member (e.g. Aunty Mabel) is a fantastic way to start. Doing your first reading for an unwilling or 'non-believer' can be a soul-diminishing activity. You'll likely lose any fledgling confidence you had and whither under negative feedback, regardless of how it's phrased. If you have a friend who already has some experience with your divination modality, this is a bonus, as they can help you out when you get stuck, and graciously look away while you furtively consult a guidebook such as this one.

Structure your sessions
It's helpful to have an adaptable structure pre-planned. A structure can get you into the right headspace and help you feel confident knowing you'll cover the key aspects for your querent. Here are some suggestions on how to structure your reading.

Try having an introductory 'patter' or pre-determined greeting to ease you and your querent into the reading. I like to start by introducing myself and asking (or confirming) the querent's name. Next, I ask the querent why they've come for a reading today, and whether they've had a reading previously. If they say 'yes', I will ask how long ago the reading was. This helps me determine if they are 'reader shopping', attempting to get a different (or the same!) answer to a certain query. I then ask if the querent if they have a specific question or if there is an area of their life they would like to focus on. Often, I'll ask my querents if they are currently in a romantic relationship, as I find this reduces the number of potential interpretations during the reading.

Regardless of any preparation work, my Tarot cards will sometimes just show what *they* feel needs to be shown, and I often share that information upfront, though of course that won't be appropriate in all sessions.

Sometimes, I receive information which doesn't seem to fit the narrative of the reading or come directly from the tool I am working with – usually a string of words or a pithy saying – and I'm not sure what it means or why it has come through. I tend to share this as an aside with the client, framing it is as something outside/beyond the tool I am using. The client is then free to decide if this 'psychic message' is relevant to them and their situation. This creates trust with the client because it shows I am not filtering the information.

Sometimes too, my intuition is a blunt instrument and my conscious mind/ego wants to filter it or soften it in some way. If I do try to find a 'nicer' way of delivering the message, I've noticed a loss of the flow/connection. It can be better to preface the clumsy words with 'This sounds a little blunt/awkward but …' and then delivering the message in a purer form.

Ultimately though, what happens during the session is your responsibility. As the diviner, you are the one that creates the container for otherworldly wisdom to flow to the querent. Do not be overly daunted. Every reading is different and will vary depending on the modality and the diviner and be as individual as the querents you read for!

Timekeeping during the session is particularly important when reading professionally, but also useful when practising your skills for friends and loved ones. If you're reading in person, rather than checking your mobile phone, it's nice to have a clock on the wall behind your querent. I prefer to set up my watch on the reading table next to a crystal or candle and other necessities like cleansing spritz so I can discretely glance at it. As part of the timekeeping process, learn how long it takes for you to fully drop into 'the zone' and the best time to begin to wrap things up.

How you end the session is just as important as the beginning, so ideally you will also have a plan for farewelling your client. To bring my readings to a close, a few minutes before the allocated time is up, I ask the querent if they have any questions or need additional clarification. Then I summarise the key points of the reading. If it is an in-person card reading, I invite the querent to take a photo of the spread. Finally, I gently disengage, wishing them all the best for the future.

Back-to-back readings
You'd be surprised at how popular you can become when you pull out a deck of cards or pendulum in the right social setting. Here are some tips if you are

planning on doing several divination readings in a row:
- ✦ Aim to be well-rested, with a receptive psyche, and in optimum health before doing multiple readings. This sounds obvious, but sometimes you might be tempted to read for everyone at the party after a few glasses of chardy.
- ✦ Allow enough time between readings to close off from one reading, re-centre, and prepare for the next. Do this by quickly cleansing/resetting your tool, standing up and having a good stretch. Talk to a friend or nearby person about some mundane matter if that works for you.
- ✦ I like to spritz between clients with a magical mix by *A Witches Apothecary*.
- ✦ Have a timekeeping device visible nearby so you can discretely monitor the time.
- ✦ Hydrate in between and during readings as required. Water is wonderful.
- ✦ Learn your reading limits. Do you get more buzzed and in-tune with each reading? Or do you become vaguer and wearier? Learn the number of consecutive readings you find manageable, bearing in mind that sometimes this knowledge is first gained by overdoing it! And then next time, roster in a break so you can relax and recover.

Distressing readings

At times, querents with complex personal situations will seek support from a diviner or spiritual practitioner rather than seeing a health care professional. Some people seek divination readings to have a sympathetic audience, and complex issues may surface during a reading.

Divinatory support works best when it respects the client's personal spiritual framework and supports their mundane efforts to create change in their lives. There are free online resources to help you to prepare for assisting querents if they experience extreme emotional distress during a reading. Have some referral options handy (such as Beyond Blue in Australia) for querents who may need additional mental and physical health care support.

Referrals to supportive resources are complex when you have an international clientele, as different countries and areas have different levels of access to support services. The internet is your friend here, as is asking the client to identify and connect with trusted individuals in their personal network who can offer on-the-ground support. Sometimes, this is a church or religious leader. It is important not to let your own cultural beliefs and perspectives interfere with what is best for the client.

Despite your best efforts and an extensive referral list, you will still experience difficult or distressing readings which trigger you emotionally. After experiencing an emotionally disturbing or distressing reading (either as diviner or querent) you need to take care of yourself. Leave the physical space and move your body. Eat and drink something or go to the toilet. Share your story but try not to get caught up in retelling the story and re-living it repeatedly. Reconnect with trusted people and loved ones and seek professional advice if needed.

Unhappy querents

Even the best readers bomb out from time to time so accept that it's likely to one day happen to you. Maybe you've hit your limit, physically or psychically? For various reasons, both magical and mundane, the strength of your psychic connection will fluctuate. Sometimes your cards or tools don't 'talk' to you and there's just nothing happening. You may need to abandon the current session, take a break, and hope things go better the next time around.

Sometimes, nothing seems to work. Other times, your querent may tell you upfront that what you are saying is rubbish. This (hopefully!) should be a rare event, but if it does happen, it's OK to stop the reading part way through, explain, apologise, and, if they are a paying client, offer a refund. No one is perfect, and we are not precision-machined tools guaranteed for reliable results every time.

Some querents come seeking a specific answer and become quite upset when your reading doesn't confirm their desired outcome. At other times, a querent may be told about something that will likely happen, but they can't assimilate that message with their existing mindset.

There's also a magical thing called time. It's only when the predicted events occur that the querent receives validation that the reading was accurate. If you have querents letting you know months (or years) down the track that the prophesised events happened, well, that's a good reading!

Refunds

What if you have spent an hour or so with a client who is paying for their reading, and you think things have gone well, then the person turns around and tells you it's a terrible reading? Next, they ask for a refund (or refuse to pay) with the rationale that nothing you have said makes sense.

This is where managing the expectations of your querent is vital. Have you been periodically checking in with your querent during the reading to see if what you are telling them resonates or connects with them? If you know that your strength is in predicting future events (of which the querent may have no current knowledge) have you explained that in advance, and emphasised it during the session?

If you feel that the demand for a refund is a deliberate ploy to avoid payment, be prepared. Have a response ready that is polite yet firm. Maybe you are fine to offer a complete refund under these circumstances. It can be a swift and effective way to cleanly end a murky interaction with a disgruntled individual. Alternatively, you may prefer to offer a half refund or no refund at all. In this case, you might like to say something like:

"I thought the reading went well. You appeared to connect with what I said and often agreed with what was discussed. I'm sorry to hear that now I've finished, you would like a refund. Unfortunately, I don't offer refunds [or am only willing to offer a half price refund] for my time and expertise."

Spooky similarities

After performing a few readings, you may sometimes notice similarities or themes emerging. You may experience a run of similar questions or topics which repeatedly emerge in your readings. These could be associated with a particular astrological transit or parallel events in your own life. Or perhaps you are tapping into a specific vein of collective experience which your clients have also connected to. Mundane level, socio-economic trends can also influence the requested topics for readings.

Be on the lookout for occasions when you are reading for someone else, and the message seems to also be about a specific situation in your own life. Yes, it happens. Perhaps it's due to the multi-layered structure of the otherworlds, or a temporary soul connection. An alternative explanation is that perhaps you aren't in a good or clear state of mind to be reading for others, as there are significant events occurring in your own life, and you haven't been able to set aside your own personal concerns. Either way, this is an interesting and thought-provoking occurrence.

Another similarity is the potential to attract a specific kind of clientele. Like does attract like. An astrologer friend with a strong 8th house invariably attracts clients with strong 8th house themes, so she knows that most of her client consultations are going to keep pointing her back to her own life themes. Because the 8th house can be heavy with themes of death, angst, and loss, she must keep her own self-care needs front of mind when she is scheduling her clients. I tend to get a lot of ambitious and/or creative people working towards a big goal, like a seat on the board or their next book, and I must watch their contagious enthusiasm doesn't inspire me to sign up for a one-way ride to Overwhelm City.

What if people keep coming back and wanting a different response?
Keep to your boundaries if this happens. You may not feel that it is appropriate to do another reading too soon after your previous reading. Or you may be completely fine about it. It comes down to your ethics and reading style. If you are charging money, there is no reason why you shouldn't request the same price for each subsequent reading. However, some readers with regular clients do offer them a discount. It's your call.

> At times, people seek a divinatory reading because they want to feel reassured, or to talk about themselves in a safe situation. Be prepared to provide support by listening to what your querents wish to share.

Professional Practicalities

Are you ready to go pro? Once you've got a sense of what makes a good reading and feel you have gained proficiency in your chosen method of divination, you may start thinking that it's time to charge money for your readings. But first things first, how do you decide when you are ready to start requesting payments? Signs include:

- ✦ There's no need to refer to the guidebook. Yes, this is a basic qualification, but it does need to be said upfront. Do you know your divination method inside out and trust your abilities?
- ✦ Friends, acquaintances, and family members (not just Aunty Mabel who dotes upon you) have provided you with genuinely positive feedback, praising your accuracy and style.
- ✦ You've sought readings from other professionals to learn and assess 'tricks of the trade' and you feel that your readings are on par with theirs.
- ✦ You have the maturity and confidence to sensitively handle complex social dynamics and challenging emotional situations.
- ✦ You are committed to protect confidential information and personal disclosures.
- ✦ You understand scheduling and basic accounting. (More about that soon.)

One thing you don't need to have before charging for readings is a piece of paper declaring you have completed a weekend course or online 'masterclass'. An easily achieved certificate isn't as valuable as the hours you spend honing your skills, improving your accuracy, or tending your interpersonal communication skills.

No matter the modality, a wise teacher will encourage students to look at a wide range of divinatory symbols and patterns and share insights with family and friends as practice. Self-taught diviners will follow the same learning trajectory. Charging money for a reading comes with responsibility and professionalism which can only be gained through experience. And there's the rub: how do you get the experience you need without having the experience you need? It's a delicate balance and a challenge not only found in the realm of divinatory practice. There comes a point when you know enough theory and the only way you are going to learn more is by 'going live' and taking a leap of faith in your own ability.

Doing business
How much should you charge? Services have varying prices, from modest for the newcomer, to premium if you have a high media profile with repeat clientele. Once you are at a stage of reasonable proficiency, try charging within the middle range. Your price may need to vary depending on your location or setting. Working at a psychic fair or setting up a market stall have different overheads to online sessions. The duration of the reading should also be reflected in the pricing.

If you are serious about being a professional diviner and intend to develop a sustainable business, it's important not to undervalue your services. On the other hand, to ensure your services are accessible and inclusive, you may also like to consider alternate pricing models (e.g. a sliding scale) or offer services with a range of price points.

Investigate your country's legal requirements for setting up a business. For example, the Australian Taxation Office offers useful information about Australian Business Numbers (ABN) and operating as a sole trader. You may also like to register a business name, though this isn't necessary up front. Usually, there are charges associated with registering a business name, though ABNs are free. If you want to trademark your business name, you'll need to consider doing this separately in different countries, due to diverse regulations and requirements.

Setting up a separate bank account will make taxation and accounting matters easier, particularly if you have significant business earnings and outgoings. Linking an online payment system such as PayPal to your bank account is also convenient for online or credit card payments.

One of the best purchases you can make if you intend to do in-person readings is an electronic device to process credit cards. For example, Square readers are available for purchase in most major Australian office or business supply stores. There are fees for each transaction, but a device to accept electronic payments is vital in many settings.

There are still people who prefer to pay for in-person readings with cash. Be prepared and have enough change available, depending on the prices of your readings.

You may also need to consider the need for upfront payments. Pre-payment is standard practice for online sessions. You may like to ask people to pre-pay at a festival or market, especially for a late timeslot on a busy day.

Consider getting public liability insurance. If you are a member of a professional organisation, they sometimes partner with insurance providers for professional indemnity. Read the fine print, and don't assume you are automatically covered for all scenarios or locations. Sometimes, event organisers will offer public liability insurance for a modest price. Another alternative is to insure yourself as a 'performer/entertainer'.

Disclaimers

Divination sessions often come with disclaimers about the reading being 'for entertainment purposes only'. This isn't because readers don't take their job seriously. It is to protect the reader from being sued by the client and is often required for insurance purposes. You may also see a statement that the divinatory consultation 'is not a substitute for specific advice from a trained professional, such as a financial advisor, lawyer, or medical practitioner'.

In this sense, divination can be thought of as akin to complementary medicine. It's not a replacement or alternative to conventional medicine (or financial and legal frameworks) but can work harmoniously side-by-side, tending to the spiritual/soul needs of the client as they navigate external realities.

> If all this talk of money and taxation and insurance has you recoiling, professional reading probably isn't for you. At least, not yet.

Venue options
Online

There are multiple ways to conduct online readings. These include live video meetings (via options such as Zoom, Teams, or Messenger), email (which may include sending a summary of the reading, transcript and/or audio file with a photo or image), or through pre-recorded video using online file sharing. Doing a live reading using a chat function (i.e. typing questions and responses) is another option.

You will need to determine how your querents will book and pay in advance of the reading. Some people like to use sites such as Etsy to facilitate bookings and payments, while others will organise money transfer via PayPal or direct bank deposit transfers.

If you get busy or want to streamline your booking process, use a calendar booking app such as Calendly, Zcal or Acuity. Look for one which helpfully converts time zones, syncs with your electronic calendar, and offers appointment reminders.

Some clients find technology difficult. A bad internet connection can also cause monumental problems and stress. Try to have a backup plan such as an 'old style' phone call if things don't go according to plan.

Online hotline – Kim's experiences

I first came across psychic hotlines as a teenager staying up late when the ads on TV started to get weird. Technology has come a long way from 1900-PSYCHIC. Although I prefer clients to book an appointment with me directly via my website, a decent percentage of my income comes via 'online walk-ins' for a large North American-based website.

I've only worked for the one company but was recruited to another Australian-based platform that turned out to be little more than a vanity project for one particularly entrepreneurial reader (who has since disappeared, of course). So, shop around for a (relatively) reputable company which respects their clientele and their readers.

The person recruiting you should assess your divination skills and ask questions about the kinds of readings you are and aren't comfortable giving (e.g., some readers prefer not to field questions about health and death). Keep in mind though that the company wants you to connect with as many clients as possible for as long as possible and if you limit your repertoire of questions, you will be a less appealing investment.

How did I find this position? By being a member of professional groups on social media – investing in your peer networks, both locally and globally/online, is an important part of professional practice – and seeing a post from someone seeking new readers for the website. I contacted them, did an interview on Skype, which other than the 'test reading' was much like any other job interview, and soon started work.

I like it because I can work from home and it fits in well around my family life, writing, and other business tasks. Content creation and promotion can often be exhausting (plus it's not my core business) so it's good to outsource that burden, at least partially, to an organisation with a marketing budget. The fast pace and high volume of readings are like reps in a gym. You'll get real good, real fast, or you'll find an alternate way of earning a living. You'll also gain insight into a wider range of clients and be asked more varied questions than you would receive in your own little patch of the world, because the internet is open to everyone. There are some long-term clients who you will develop excellent rapport with and get to know over a long period; seeing their lives change for the better is rewarding.

The downsides include not forming a direct relationship with your clientele. You will get regulars but unless they are motivated and resourceful, they are unlikely to find your website. Your contract with the company will include a clause which prevents you from poaching their clients. Some days you'll be available online and get tumbleweeds instead of clients, so I would caution you not to trustingly put all your eggs in someone else's basket. The readings themselves are not as 'well contained' because they are per minute. Sometimes they are ridiculously short. Other times you are 80 minutes in and wishing you'd listened to that fleeting urge to pee or eat before you'd accepted the call/chat.

The exchange rate between currencies fluctuates and international transfer fees bite. If you aren't techy, don't bother because you'll need to be able to set up various platforms and troubleshoot connectivity issues from time to time.

Speaking more than one language is a definite bonus and helps attract clients, so be sure to mention that in your bio. You'll need a head shot – preferably one of your own head but not necessarily. An unusual number of my online colleagues wear dark-rimmed spectacles in their photos and sometimes I wonder if this gets them more clients. You can give yourself a mystical alias but I list my real name so people can find my website and discover books such as this one.

Face-to-face

There are many opportunities for professional face-to-face readings. Some independent bookshops, cafes, and crystal shops have a reading space available, sometimes with a roster of practitioners. This is an easy option for the new reader, as the store will assist with marketing and the basic requirements of a table, chairs, electricity and booking system. Some reading spaces are beautifully appointed. Generally, the store will keep a percentage of the fee to cover their costs.

If that's something you'd like to do, make an appointment to speak to the owner or manager. Be prepared to undertake a trial reading or two, so they can ascertain your skill level, reading style and communication abilities. Be patient as it may take a while for you to build up a reputation. Your first clients are likely to be curious walk-ins who don't pre-book.

You may feel comfortable doing readings in your own home, particularly if there is a separate entrance available for clients. There are security risks associated with this option, but there are also advantages – there's no commute and you don't have an additional financial outlay for space. You can also permanently set up a beautiful, personalised area dedicated to readings.

Perhaps the most common place to do face-to-face readings in Australia is at a psychic fair or market. These occur all around the county, and often there is an organiser (or a team) who runs multiple events. Organisers will take a percentage of your income, as they provide marketing, booking, and equipment. At other markets, you need to pay the upfront cost of hiring the stall space and keep all income.

Market stall – practical suggestions from Sandra

I love to offer readings at markets, particularly outdoor markets in fine weather. It's fun, interesting, and can be extremely busy. Generally, for outdoor markets, you'll need to provide your own 3 x 3 metre tent/canopy, though some venues do offer these for hire at an extra cost.

Be prepared with super strong tent pegs (not the nasty flimsy bendy pegs some canopies come with) or have alternative weights for venues where tent pegs are not allowed. You will need to anchor that canopy securely. Trust me on this. Having my tent blow away mid-reading was a memorable experience, but one I'd prefer not to repeat.

If you have an outdoor stall, you'll also need to consider wall hangings for privacy, and to stop the wind from whisking things away. Other market stall or event items you may need are:

- *Signage.* You can hand paint a sign, write on a whiteboard, or order a banner from a printing company. Pull-up banners are ubiquitous at some markets, though you will need to keep them inside your designated stall area. If you get a hanging banner, it's well worth the extra cost to get eyelets included, so you can tie these to posts. A glossy A4 poster inside a clear frame is a great starting option, before committing to a professionally printed sign.
- *Table and chairs.* Some organisers will provide these for a small fee. Otherwise, bring your own, preferably ones which are light to carry. It's not a lot of fun lugging a 20 kg table back to the car park at the end of the day.
- *Trolley.* Some people like to use a trolley rather than carry items, but I'm a fan of light-weight items and packing things in small boxes that can be carried up and down stairs, rather than waiting half an hour to

catch the only functioning lift with all the other market stall holders who are also packing up at the same time.
- *A helper.* Having other people on the stall to help with bookings and chat to potential clients is invaluable. Thank your helper by buying them coffee and/or food.
- *A printed booking sheet.* Include time slots and spaces to write names and phone numbers as well as payment types. It's easy to lose track of times and clients when you are busy.
- *Business cards.* These are surprisingly cheap to purchase. I prefer the single-sided option, so I can scribble information (like the appointment time) on the blank side.
- *Hand wash and/or wipes* for grubby hands, or to refresh between readings.
- *Water and snacks* in case you get busy and can't leave the stall.
- *Decorations* to jazz up your stall, like tablecloths, fairy lights, and novelty items. Get creative! (There's more advice in the following section on marketing.)
- *Odds and ends box* with scissors, bulldog clips, sticky tape, rope, breath freshener, pain relief medications (vital for us more mature readers who experience various aches and pains), notepad and pens.
- *Electronic money transfer device.* Don't forget a battery pack and charging cables to keep this device as well as your phone and/or computer charged.
- *Cash* to cover differences in payment.

Marketing

Arguably, marketing and promoting your own business is the worst part of being a professional reader. While planning your marketing strategy you may experience feelings of imposter syndrome or extreme resistance and just want it all to go away. Remember, perfection is the enemy of good enough. Don't put too much pressure on yourself to have the ideal setup the first time you read professionally. Otherwise, you may spend hours overthinking it, rather than just doing it!

With your branding and marketing concepts, start simple. What's your favourite colour? What do you plan on wearing or is there a certain clothing style you prefer? What resources do you have at hand? Are you comfortable with having your face being your brand, or would you prefer a logo or image?

Start with what you have, and then evolve your style as you become more comfortable and have a better idea of what your 'brand' is.

You are unlikely to be an expert at all things marketing and that's OK. Some of us love social media but are terrible at styling a market stall. Or vice versa. Allow yourself to experiment with multiple concepts. I've had a range of banners made (depending on how I felt at the time) and have used too-small white sheets to inadequately cover tables. I usually wear whatever I feel like wearing on the day, although one day I forgot my chosen market outfit and had to wear my smelly 'setup clothes' all day. Fortunately, talented, crafty friends such as Scarlet and Merewyn vastly improve on my (pathetic) styling attempts.

At the other end of the continuum is a witch friend from southeast Queensland who totally rocks her branding. She has a colour theme of black and purple and uses these throughout her product range. Every market, she dresses carefully in the same colours, and wears a distinctive hat. Her face (and hat) feature in her banners. She's also got a cool logo in her brand colours. This is highly effective marketing – she's clearly identifiable wherever she goes, in-person and online.

Social media is an important marketing channel – and could be more important than a purpose-built website when you first start out. Currently, the biggest social media sites are Facebook/Meta, Instagram, Twitter, and TikTok. Each site has its own demographic, audience, and demands. You need to find what works best for your style of interaction and your potential clientele. As a starting point, creating a page on Facebook/Meta is handy, as you can use this to host information about your services, rather than immediately investing in your own website.

To help build your public profile, ask people to leave a review on your social media, Google business page, or your website at the end of the reading. Good reviews are critical to business success. Offer the querent your business card when reading in person as a prompt to write a review or suggest you to a friend. Word of mouth referrals are a wonderful way to grow your business.

Being the Querent

As a client/querent, preparation is key to creating an optimal experience during your divination session. As a querent, you are always the expert on your life. Take on board the guidance and suggestions provided by your diviner but do not hand over responsibility. And certainly, don't hand over your money for curse-breaking services which are invariably a scam.

If the reader is saying things that you find upsetting or you are not yet ready to hear or address, you always have the power and authority to bring the session to an end. It is your reading after all. You are not bound to follow the advice or suggestions of the diviner and always retain your free will and agency to make life choices which are appropriate for you.

In advance, try to have a level of engagement with your own life, and identify goals or areas of interest to explore before your divination session. Asking for 'a general reading' will give you a general reading and likely lead to disappointment. The request for a general reading may also make it more difficult for the diviner to tune into the vast array of possibilities floating around in the ether. If you're happy to drift, the Universe will help you do it.

That said, if you are feeling lost, confused, and directionless, tell your diviner upfront as this is a specific issue which can be explored and potentially resolved through divination.

If you ask a reader about the lottery numbers, they will tell you "It doesn't work like that" and roll their eyes, inwardly if you are lucky. If they are particularly tired and you are particularly persistent, they will give you some random numbers. These numbers will not work any better than numbers you choose yourself because it really doesn't work like that. If it did, your diviner would be sipping cocktails mixed by someone sexy rather than generating random numbers like a computerised fairy godmother.

Ask questions that matter. If you are short of money, don't ask about lottery tickets. Instead, ask how you can alleviate your strained financial situation.

> An effective divination session requires trust and openness to forge a quality connection between client and reader.

Good and bad readings

This brings us to the question of whether there are good divination readings and bad divination readings, and how you tell the difference. While it's ultimately down to you as querent to determine whether you have had an excellent or a poor-quality reading, here's my list of pet peeves and pathways to perfection.

Signs of a bad reading

- The reader tries to energetically suck the querent's soul into their aura. This kind of reader has an intense and hypnotic vibe, leaves lengthy silences, and stares deeply into the client's eyes. Watch for an uncomfortable sense of pressure or a disconcerting non-physical pushing sensation.
- The reader offers a vast range of different options, instead of singular clarity or, if there are multiple possibilities, appropriate assistance with decision making.
- It can also be troubling when the reader only offers one precise outcome, which can make the client feel like they've received a cookie-cutter reading or been put into a stereotypical box.
- The reader asks too many questions and then uses the responses to guide every step of their reading. (If this happens, I adopt an enigmatic gaze and nod vaguely. I like my readers to do the work.)
- The querent leaves the reading feeling even more puzzled and perplexed than before. Huh?
- When a Tarot reader is charging money and has a book called *How to Read Tarot Cards for Really Stupid Dummies* on their table.

Signs of a good reading

- The reader includes some verifiable information about the past or current circumstances to validate they have made a genuine connection. That way I'm going to trust them more when they tell me about future possibilities.

+ The reader checks in from time to time to verify accuracy or to see if the querent has questions. This should be done for confirmation rather than requesting a life history.
+ There are sensitive discussions regarding situations which are complex or potentially distressing (if these arise).
+ The reading includes some insights about future circumstances and possibilities. If this doesn't occur, I feel like I've wasted my time and hard-earned money by only being told about the current status quo.
+ The reading goes for 30–60 minutes. My personal preference is 45 minutes. Longer divination sessions are exhausting for both diviner and querent. The surplus information shared isn't necessarily better quality and only so much can be assimilated at a time. If there is more to explore, it is better to have split sessions.
+ The querent walks away feeling empowered with useful insights about their life.

> Divination should make living your life easier.
> Ethical diviners want to help you live your best life.

References and Bibliography

Bardon, Franz. *Initiation into Hermetics*. New Leaf Distributing Co Inc, 2016.
Buckland, Raymond. *Buckland's Complete Book of Witchcraft*. USA, Llewellyn Publications, 1986 (1997 version).
Campbell, Joseph. *The Hero with a Thousand Faces*. 3rd edition. New World Library, 2012.
Crowley, Aleister. *Magick, Liber ABA: Book IV*. 2nd Revised ed. Edition. Red Wheel/Weiser, 2005.
Cunningham, Scott. *Cunningham's Encyclopedia of Magical Herbs*. USA. Llewellyn Publications,1985
Duquette, Lon Milo, *Enochian Vision Magick : An Introduction and Practical Guide to the Magick of Mr. John Dee and Edward Kelley*. Weiser Books, 2008.
Eason, Cassandra. *A Little Bit of Palmistry*. New York USA. Sterling Ethos, 2018.
Ellison, Robert. *Ogham: The Secret Language of the Druids*. ADF Publishing, 2008.
Fenton, Sasha. *Super Tarot*. The Aquarian Press, 1991.
Greenhalgh, Sandra. *Druid Wisdom Oracle*. Byrning Tyger, 2019.
Herb Rally – herbal monographs online at https://www.herbrally.com/monographs
Hoffman, Enid. *Hands: A Complete Guide to Palmistry*. Schiffer Pub Ltd, 1997.
Houlding, Deborah. *The Houses: Temples of the Sky*. Wessex Astrologer, 1998.
Lehman, Lee. *The Book of Rulerships: Keywords from Classical Astrology*. Whitford Press, 1993.
McManus, Damian. *Guide to Ogam* (Maynooth Monograph 4) Maynooth: An Sagart, 1991.
MacNeill, Duanaire Finn. *The Book of the Lays of Finn*. London. Irish Texts Society, 1908.
Mirriam Webster dictionary, online at https://www.merriam-webster.com/
Plant.net – plant identification app
Shakespeare, William. *Macbeth,* England. Wordsworth Classics, 1992.
Tanet, Alexandra, *Living Witchery: Coven*, Byrning Tyger, 2021
Tanet, Fairminer & Greenhalgh. *Living Witchery Beginner Witch Guide*. Australia. Byrning Tyger, 2021.

The Book of Taliesin – LLyfr Taliesin (Peniarth MS 2), 14th century. Online at: https://www.library.wales/discover-learn/digital-exhibitions/manuscripts/the-middle-ages/book-of-taliesin

The Book of Ballymote – Leabhar Bhaile an Mhóta, 14th century.

The Scholar's Primer – Auraicept na N-Éces translated by George Calder, Edinburgh, John Grant 1917. http://archive.org/details/auraicept00calduoft/

The Yellow Book of Lecan – Leabhar Buidhe Lecain, 14th century.

Webster, Richard. *Palm Reading for Beginners*. USA. Llewellyn Publications, 2000.

Acknowledgements and Credits

A book is a creation which involves many beings. We are grateful for the support from our families, friends, and spirit-kin. Our appreciation is boundless. In this section we'd also like to mention some extra special people.

- Cheryl (Rhianna) you are so missed. Vale (2022), but you are never too far away from our memories. And thanks for pushing up *Living Witchery Beginner Witch Guide* to be number 1 bestseller on Amazon on the day of your funeral. We know it was you!
- Gillian for beta reading yet again! You are a Goddess.
- Vale Tess (2022), we wish that you were still with us to share your wisdom and pick up those fiendish spelling errors.
- Elkie White and Kacey Stephenson, thanks for your feedback regarding the Ogham chapter.
- Sam from Three Fates Apothecary for casting your discerning astrological eye over the horary chapter.
- Luke from Fleetfoot Photography for the back cover image.
- Linda Marson for Tarot images.
- Sandra Greenhalgh for interior images, inspired by photos by
    - Scarlet Paige (Australian Green Man)
    - Lisa-jane (black mirrors)
    - Caroline Tully (Tarot reader)

www.ingramcontent.com/pod-product-compliance
Lightning Source LLC
Chambersburg PA
CBHW051537010526
44107CB00064B/2754